Original Truth

SHARPENING YOUR SWORD OF CONSCIOUSNESS AND SPIRIT
USING MARTIAL ARTS & PHILOSOPHY

LAK LOI

ORIGINAL TRUTH

SHARPENING YOUR SWORD OF CONSCIOUSNESS AND SPIRIT
USING MARTIAL ARTS & PHILOSOPHY

LAK LOI

DEDICATIONS

FIRSTLY, I WOULD LIKE TO DEDICATE THIS BOOK TO MY GOOD
FRIEND AND LEADING AUTHORITY ON BRUCE LEE AND HIS MARTIAL
ART AND PHILOSOPHY, JEET KUNE DO – ANDREW STATON.

He has always gone out of his way to bless me with success in sharing
my message of the mental and spiritual side of Bruce Lee's teachings
of the martial way, in addition to Bruce's physical teachings.

Secondly, I would like to dedicate this book to my good friend and founder of
World of Martial Arts TV and Magazine, Will Henshaw, who trusted me and
gave me a platform upon which to share my message.

PEACE, RESPECT & LOVE

X

CREDITS

Nathan Cole Visual Communication Ltd
for the front and back cover images and book formatting,
www.nathancole.me

Artwork from WordSwag™, Pixabay™ and Shutterstock™

DISCLAIMER

The author and publisher have made every effort to ensure that the information and advice in this book helps to serve the reader to create positive life changes.

The author and publisher do not assume and hereby disclaim any liability to any party for any loss, damage, disruption or death caused by the information, advice, errors or omissions, whether they exist from negligence, accident or any other cause.

The views expressed in this book are solely those of the author, and do not reflect the views of the publisher or any other parties involved in the production of this book. Readers should take the content of this book as simply the author's personal experience and humble opinion, and not as an intention to cause offence or upset in any way whatsoever.

The author advises the reader to take full responsibility and control for their actions, health and safety and to know their limits when undertaking any of the advice and engaging in any of the exercises, drills and activities described in this book. If the reader has any medical conditions, then they should seek consent from their physician before engaging in any physical activity and ensure that any equipment is safe and well maintained. They should avoid taking any risks beyond their level of experience, ability, aptitude, training and comfort.

COPYRIGHT

First published 2020 by Rowanvale Books Ltd.

The Gate
Keppoch Street
Roath
Cardiff
CF24 3JW

www.rowanvalebooks.com

A CIP catalogue record for this book is available from the British Library.
ISBN: 978-1-912655-86-1

CONTENTS

THE ANCIENT SECRET
OF MARTIAL ARTS

THE ORIGINAL TRUTH REVEALED

EAST MEETS WEST

ACROSS THE WORLD, EASTERN MARTIAL ARTS MASTERS FROM INDIA, CHINA AND JAPAN, AS WELL AS TRIBAL WARRIOR CHIEFS OF INDIGENOUS TRIBES OF THE AMERICAS AND AFRICA (TO NAME BUT A FEW PLACES), HAVE CLOSELY GUARDED THE ANCIENT SECRET OF MARTIAL ARTS.

They all knew this profound wisdom, and many say the secret travelled West from the mysterious East with the likes of an Indian Buddhist monk called Bodhidharma (to name one of many greats who spread this enlightened wisdom), who became famous for founding Shaolin Kung Fu.

What they all had in common was their approach to martial arts as a holistic way of living, not just a way of kicking and punching your way through troubles when times get tough.

They all followed the same process, which went…

- Heal your spirit, so you can heal others' spirits.

- Heal your mind, so you can heal others' minds.

- Heal your body, so you can heal others' bodies.

- Only then were you qualified to learn combative motion to hurt others for 'just' causes only.

The firm belief among all these ancient masters was that when there is a problem in your spirit, it manifests itself in your mind as limiting beliefs, thoughts and actions. When there is a problem in your mind, it will eventually manifest itself in your body as an ailment or illness. I like to think of the human body as a dashboard. When your car's dashboard shows low fuel, high coolant temperature or an engine management problem, you know something is wrong under the hood that needs urgent attention before the car breaks down. Similarly, our bodies are dashboards for the spirit and mind, and when a rash, cold or cough appear, it is just a light trying to tell us something needs fixing under our hoods before our bodies come crashing down with sickness. Therefore, the big idea is to heal your spirit to collapse the chain of problems through the spirit, mind and body.

A good friend of mine, a Hakko-Ryu Jujutsu practitioner Jerry Tardi, once told me:

'If you can break it,
You should know how to make it.'

Hence, you have to learn to self-heal first. Martial arts are just another form of self-help. I like to say:

'There are many roads to Edinburgh.'

The greatest masters of all time were first and foremost healers and renowned medicine men and women who were looked up to as leaders of their communities and tribes, for healing of daily ills and thereafter, with sound advice and wisdom, to protect and preserve the community. One of my good friends, Tom McGrath, once told me:

'You cannot give something away
If you don't have it in the first place.'

Unfortunately, we have it all back to front in the West. We are very much stuck in the body, if not for vanity then because we are fixated on the prowess of physical violence. The glorification of combat sports such as cage fighting, professional boxing and wrestling has drawn us further away from the truth. We are so stuck in the body; we have lost sight of the bigger picture.

The ancient secret I am about to reveal has been deeply buried as a result of this, and seldom is it taught in martial arts schools because of a lack of understanding and the commercial lure of the physical elements of martial arts, an understandable desire for financial gain by giving customers what they want rather than what they need: to heal themselves, others, the planet and build strong, loving communities to protect and to serve one another in unison.

WHAT'S IN A NAME?

The secret has always been there right in front of our faces. It has been in the name 'martial arts' itself all this time. But the problem is, we often misunderstand what 'martial arts' means. Often, people will consider 'martial arts' to just mean 'war like', putting an emphasis on physical combat, but there's much more to this than you realise. Let me explain the true meaning of martial arts...

1. The first side of the coin is when we **heal** the spirit, mind and body – this is to **create,** or the **'art'** part of martial art.

2. The second side of the coin is when we have to **hurt** using combat, for 'just' causes only – this is to **destroy**, or the **'martial'** part of martial art.

When we recognise and start to understand the two sides of this indivisible coin, we can start to become whole, healed and happy

through the process of cultivating ourselves, or what I call
Self Mastery. This allows us to heal ourselves so we can heal others
and Mother Earth. This is the true meaning of martial arts – life.

Figure 1: The true meaning of 'martial art'

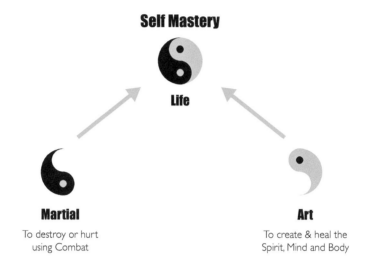

As I like to say:

'Hurt people hurt people,
Healed people heal people.'

Martial arts give us tools to understand our body, and by investigating
what is happening inside us and comparing it to what is happening
outside in nature, we are able to realise the laws of nature inside and
out are interdependent. The two parts of the whole are known as
the **macrocosm** (big – the universe) and the **microcosm** (small –
the human being), and the two are intertwined. Everything inside us
we can project outwardly from something unexplainable that comes
from deep within us (spirit), which translates into a thought (mind),
which we convert into physical action (body) to manifest it in our
reality (life).

REVEALING THE SECRET

The ancient secret of martial arts was discovered by the Taoists, who studied the effects of naturally occurring universal processes upon human nature. By observing nature and investigating the effects of its energy upon and within the human body, the Taoists traced nature's energy back to its source. They used **meditation** to make this 'expedition'. The search led them to the discovery of a primordial void, a condition of nothingness. This void, recognised to have been the state of things at the beginning of all creation, was given the name **Wu Chi,** meaning 'Original Source' or the 'Great Emptiness'. This is depicted in Taoist art as an empty circle.

Figure 2: The ultimate outcome of the martial arts process
is to connect to the 'Original Source' or 'Wu Chi'

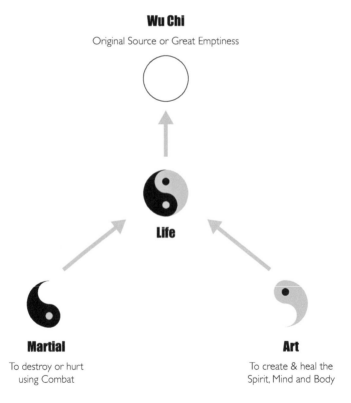

Wu Chi
Original Source or Great Emptiness

Life

Martial
To destroy or hurt
using Combat

Art
To create & heal the
Spirit, Mind and Body

The energies born from Wu Chi are the main forces that sustain our lives: universal energy (stars, planets, galaxies and multi-verses), human plane energy (cosmic particles or stellar dust), and earth energy (water, plants and animals). These forces work together in harmony to sustain all existence, and it is our job, through cultivating self-mastery by learning martial arts to understand our body, mind and spirit, to connect to the Original Source. This is the biggest secret of martial arts that has been hidden all this time, and everything else along the way has merely served as a distraction. As Bruce Lee famously said:

> 'It's like a finger pointing away to the moon.
> Don't concentrate on the finger
> Or you will miss all that heavenly glory.'

Now this is easy to say, but hard to do. It takes years of practising martial arts to ascend your understanding to the level of connecting to the Original Source. You must:

- Physically master martial arts techniques to be able to defend yourself against harm (body).

- Cultivate your mind so you are emotionally resilient to cope with daily life challenges without resorting to physical violence (mind).

- Cultivate your inner compass and be able to listen to your intuition and energy to make sound, conscious decisions (spirit).

Only then will you be able to go deeper within to connect to the Original Source, through deep meditation.

Now, there are different types of meditation, from sitting to standing to moving – which is exactly what martial arts is, a **moving meditation**. To connect to the Original Source, you need to find someone that has made that connection in the first place, so they can give it to you, so you too can **connect to Wu Chi.**

Remember, once you have discovered your gift, you have an obligation to give it away.

GAME OF DEATH
– PART 1

IT'S LIKE RIDING A BIKE

HAZARD FIXATION

Martial artists are very similar to motorcyclists. Let me elaborate…

When motorcyclists learn how to ride a motorcycle, one of the first things they learn is the vital idea of 'hazard fixation.' That is, if you focus your gaze on something, that is where your motorcycle is going to go. So, if you're looking at a pothole, thinking, 'I need to avoid that pothole,' guess what? You'll ride straight into it. If you're looking at a lamp post, thinking, 'I need to avoid that lamp post,' guess what? You're going to wrap your bike around it.

Martial arts are exactly the same as riding a motorcycle.
Bear with me…

GETTING PUNCHED IN THE FACE

During sparring, have you ever thought, 'I do not want to get punched in the face?' And then there it is… BOOM!!!
You get punched square in the face!

EMBARRASSED BY YOUR EMBARRASSMENT

During sparring, have you ever thought, 'I do not want to embarrass myself?' And then there it is… HOLY CRAP!!! Your opponent bursts into a flurry of strikes, putting you into a corner, punching, kicking and hurting your ego.

WINNING IS EVERYTHING

During sparring, have you ever thought, 'I have to win,' and you start premeditating moves and combos to defeat your opponent? And then there it is NOT… The opportunity to play out your scenarios never comes because the fight doesn't go like you imagined, and you start to get really frustrated, angry, rigid and tense, leading to the further demise of your performance.

And so it is: whatever you fix your gaze on tends to happen even though your intention was to avoid it.

RIDING A BIKE

It's like riding a bike.

When you first start to learn how to ride a bike,
you have to figure out:

- How to sit on the bike,

- How to grip the handlebars,

- How to distribute your weight to find your balance,

- How to put your feet on the pedals,

- How to propel the bike forwards,

- How to stay upright in a straight line,

- How to steer the bike safely without high-siding or low-siding,

- How to brake carefully so you stop safely without skidding, crashing or going over the handlebars,

…until your trainer lets go of your seat and you don't even know it, and you're doing it all yourself, oblivious that IT'S ALL YOU. There is a moment of complete freedom, where all your thoughts have died and there is nothing left but you in the flow, feeling the breeze… THAT'S IT! That's a moment of 'Learning the Art of Dying', often referred to as 'Living in the Now' and 'Being Present'.

Bruce Lee summed this up beautifully when he said:

'To understand and live now,
There must be a dying to everything of yesterday,
Die continually to every newly gained experience,
Be in a state in choiceless awareness of what is.'

At first your motion is very rigid, mechanical and robotic. Six months down the line, you're not thinking about any of the above anymore. You're more concerned with having fun riding your bike with your friends: you're engaged in fun banter, enjoying the adventure and excited about where this journey is going to take you! You attain a fluidity and presence in your actions without any conscious thought, not thinking about the past or the future, just enjoying that moment in time.

The best part of riding a bike is once you've got it, you can pick up a bicycle one, five, ten years from now, and you'll still know how to ride it perfectly well.

IT DOES NOT HIT, IT HITS ALL BY ITSELF

And so it is, when you stop thinking about your opponent's strikes and allow yourself the freedom to see them coming without looking, you respond intelligently (by evading, defending or countering them) as a simple reflex, being quicker and more fluid.

THERE IS NO OPPONENT

When you stop thinking about your opponent… you start to become one with your opponent and treat sparring like a dance, but a dance performed elegantly. When your opponent advances, you retreat; when he retreats, you advance; and when you want to open a window to strike, you know exactly when and how.

WINNING IS NOTHING

When you stop thinking you have to win… you can start to accept defeat and loss. Then all there is left to do is to DO THE BEST YOU CAN! And you instantly feel relieved of any pressure and are liberated from any attachment to the outcome, satisfied in the thought that you gave it your best shot.

HAZARD UN-FIXATION

And you start to realise, as you practise 'The Art of Dying,' that you're killing all the notions that trapped you in those moments of 'hazard fixation'. It is a process of 'hazard un-fixation'.

Bruce Lee put it perfectly when he said:

'Like everyone else,
You want to learn the way to win,
But never to accept the way to lose,
To accept defeat.

To learn to die is to be liberated from it.
So when tomorrow comes,
You must free your ambitious mind, and
Learn the art of dying.'

DYING EVERY DAY

'Dying every day' does not refer to our physical demise but is rather a metaphor for something different altogether.

To be clear, the 'Game of Death' is not teaching us to kill anything or anyone outside of us. Rather, it is a killing of unresourceful thoughts, behaviours and attachments within us that no longer serve us and are holding us back from living our best life and putting our best side forwards.

I like to say:

> 'Happy people don't have the best of everything.
> They make everything the best with what they have.'

It is a release of all the strain and tension in your life caused by attachment (to not getting punched in the face, to winning, to embarrassment), so your life becomes buoyant, you get into your flow, and move gracefully through it.

Bruce Lee said:

> 'Drop and dissolve inner blockage,
> A conditioned mind is never a free mind.
> Wipe away and dissolve all its experience and be born afresh.'

And just like that, **Play the 'Game of Death' so you can Start Living.** Remember, it's like riding a bike.

TAKE ACTION AND MASTER YOUR LIFE

LETTING GO

1. Identify areas in your life where you are straining and have tension.

2. Identify what you are attached to that is causing your strain and tension.

3. Think what you can do to ease and/or eventually relieve all the strain and tension.

4. Then do those things with a congruency and ecology with yourself, other sentient beings and Mother Earth, so you can live in the now, become present and liberate yourself.

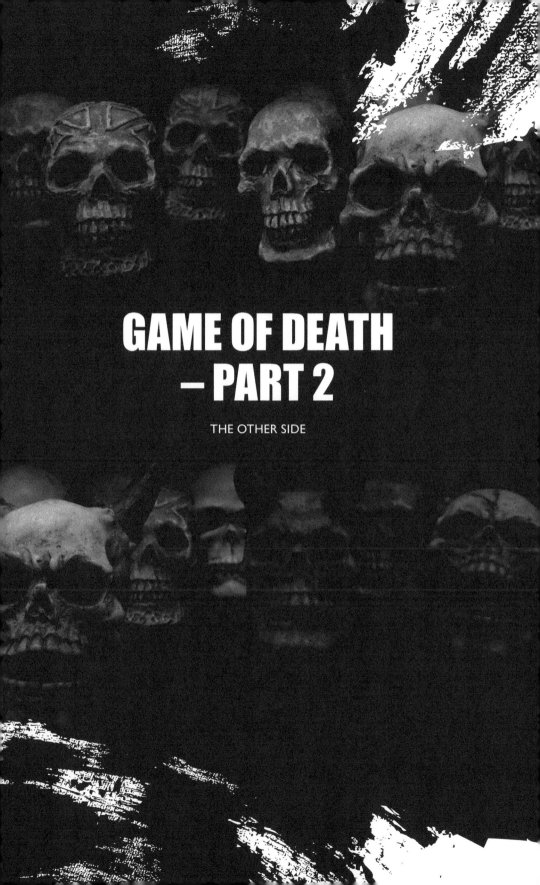

GAME OF DEATH – PART 2

THE OTHER SIDE

DARK SIDE OF DEATH

In Western society, we are conditioned to fear death as doom: dark, dreary and dangerous, and we are often scared to talk about it.

Death is generally perceived as suffering, used as a punishment for social order and conditioning, with dreadful dualistic consequences – trapping us in this lifetime to tirelessly do good to reach heaven, in constant fear of ending up in hell if we don't.

As Franklin D. Roosevelt famously said:

> 'The only thing we have to fear,
> Is fear itself.'

Our lives are filled with struggle between good and evil, for both live within us. The journey is not outside of us, but within. It is every person's right to choose the path they wish to take. We can choose to allow the compassionate and loving side of us to grow and flourish, regardless of what is happening around us, or we can decide to be controlled by negativity and fear. Be very clear, there is no right or wrong path. This is what it means to have free will.

CHOOSING BIRTH

In ancient and indigenous cultures, such as in South America, India, Africa and the Far East, there is a strong belief that we choose our own parents before we are born. We choose what experience we want to get out of life so we can learn the lessons necessary for us to evolve spiritually, so we can reveal our true authentic highest self and eventually return home to our Original Truth.

Everyone we've ever met, every experience we've ever had, have all been serving to reveal to us who we really are.

And when we miss or choose to ignore the lessons life serves us, either because we are veering off our path, distracted by all the dazzling lights along the way, or too blind to see, then life will serve us more severe lessons to help us to notice and see more clearly – what I call 'spiritual nudges'.

So, as we go on our own journeys, we should not try and duplicate someone else's but rather learn how to:

'Be yourself,
To reveal yourself.'

Your birth right as a human being is freedom of choice. The ultimate choice is the one between life and death. A loss of identity can bring you to this point and influence you to choose death. But remember, before birth, as a soul, you choose life and to come to Earth to fulfil your destiny here.

Every being has a destiny. We are all connected to the great web of life, and therefore every being on this Earth is sacred and important. You have taken human form to carry out the promises made before you entered this body, to the many people you will come into contact with in this lifetime, in order to have the choice to end your karma with them.

Time does not exist, for it is a human construct. Although our physical bodies disintegrate, our essence cannot die. It only takes on new forms that allow us to understand different experiences in different ways. Each lifetime has the potential to lead us closer to the Original Truth. And the experience of life is not the destination but the journey, the evolution of the soul. All human beings are on this journey to the Self, to enlightenment, and we are all at different stages of this journey. The people who will come and go in your life all need to meet you for their own growth, and you need them for yours. We are all connected by this one destiny – to awaken and realise our inherent divinity.

If you decide to walk into the light now (commit suicide), it is the law of nature that you must return to this Earth, but your suffering will be multiplied a hundredfold, for there is no escape from destiny, no escape from karma. If you choose life, you will fulfil your karma, your promise to these souls in this lifetime. If you choose death, you will need to return again and again for many more thousands of years.

The only way to be free of suffering is to find out who you truly are, and then BE it in order to be free. With this wisdom, you must now make your decision.

EMBRACING DIS-EASE

Dis-ease is the only real wake-up call to start living.

When we are attached to illnesses, we only focus on the dis-ease. We forget to see life as a journey where everything is flowing and in motion, so illness and dis-ease are actually opportunities for growth.

Dis-ease is the spirit's way of expressing that it is unhappy and in pain, and that it can no longer be ignored. Most people become distressed by illness, and this only increases the suffering because our fear of death causes us to fear dis-ease. We have been taught to believe that death is a punishment, and if we are good people we will not get sick or we will be cured. It is time we start to embrace death and accept it as part of the inevitable experience of life. Illness is a chance to make life changes, to start really living. It gives us the opportunity to remember what is important in our lives, to follow our dreams, to heal old wounds and say goodbye. Illness empowers the spirit to be heard and to show the way to a more fulfilling life, for however long that is.

EASING DIS-EASE

Only you can heal yourself – when you choose to, that is.
I like to say:

> 'All help
> Is self-help.'

So, what does it mean to heal?

Even when you are sick, you can heal. When we are truly happy with our lives and everything in them, and see everything is love, only then are we healed, regardless of whether our bodies are dying from wear and tear and/or old age.

We need to learn how to love ourselves, others and Mother Earth – only then does the dis-ease of spirit heal.

KILLING FOR SURVIVAL

We are all born of and belong to Mother Earth. If that is the case, then we are all one, aren't we?

Every animal or fish we kill means there is one fewer of us. Hunting teaches us how we rely on one another for survival – what we call the 'food chain'. If we create a weak link in the chain, it is sure to break, isn't it?

It is not the killing that is important, it is the intent with which we sacrifice an animal or fish that makes the difference. Intention is the key to every action. If you kill an animal or fish with honour and gratitude, then the animal does not die in vain, rather it gives its life for food and sustenance. A wise hunter never kills more than he needs.

In the West, animals and fish are farmed and killed indiscriminately. Their flesh is wasted, and their souls do not understand why they gave up their lives. Western society has lost its connection with Mother Earth and the animal kingdom, and we must wake up and realise we all have a part to play. When an animal dies in fear because of the 'human condition' for greed and profits, then we absorb that fear trapped in the flesh we consume, and we become sick.

Similarly, you may argue, "If you are a vegetarian, then why are you killing plants?" The answer is really simple... We are all here to serve one another to raise our consciousness. A plant that wants to raise its consciousness by being consumed by a human will be easily digestible, like fruits, vegetables, herbs and spices. Those plants that don't want humans to consume them are poisonous and cause us harm, such as nettles and cacti.

Similarly, if someone puts you or a loved one in harm's way, is it OK to kill them if there is no other choice? The simple truth is you would do whatever you think is necessary at that given moment in time to survive.

BLOOD BINDING LIFE AND DEATH

In the Peruvian Amazon jungle, shamanic tribes consider menstruation an auspicious time for women. It is a time for women to reconnect with themselves and Mother Earth. A time for resting and re-energising.

It is a time to give thanks for the blood that binds life and death together. It is a time to purify a woman's body of a life not meant to be. The menstrual blood is even used to cure feminine ailments.

In Western society, this special relationship between women and Mother Earth has been lost. These rites, rituals and relationships have been lost, not passed from mother to daughter in celebration of being a divine feminine, rather deemed a gross sanitary inconvenience.

DYING AND LIVING SIMULTANEOUSLY

Every moment is an opportunity for a new possibility.

With every decision we make, we are choosing who we are going to be by giving life to that thing that needs to be born in us, and at the same time, who we are not going to be anymore by killing that thing that needs to die within us.

It is our opportunity to:

> 'Choose love.
> Choose liberation.'

As the Dalai Lama said:

> 'A heart full of love and compassion is the main source of Inner strength, willpower, happiness and mental tranquillity.'

At the same time, we start to realise how death and life co-exist and complement one another, as life is the process of separation, exploration and reunion – a oneness.

Dying every moment, you get closer to death, which brings you closer to living and being truly alive.

LEARN THE ART OF DYING

Chinese martial arts philosophy believes in the wonderful idea of 'Learning the Art of Dying'.

Buddha even taught this lesson when he said:

> 'The root of all suffering
> Is attachment.'

Only once this lesson is learned can you be totally free. Shiva explains the true meaning of *Nirvana* as:

> 'Dying at every moment,
> But every moment I was closer to death,
> I was alive.'

That is a dying of feeling, hearing, seeing, talking, tasting, smelling and thinking. Becoming sense-less to become sense-full and alive.

It is like when you go into a competition fight with:

- The attachment to winning.

- The attachment to the embarrassment of getting punched in the face and what your mates think.

- The attachment to the fear of losing.

What if you went into the fight accepting defeat, accepting embarrassment, accepting loss? Then what is left?

Simply put, just **DO THE BEST YOU CAN,** freely without any attachment, and see how effortlessly you **GET INTO THE FLOW.** Then death of your attachments becomes a **CELEBRATION.** That's how you 'Learn the Art of Dying', by letting go of your attachments.

Once you have embraced death and have become comfortable with it, you can slowly step into your true authentic highest self – where your servitude to others becomes selfless, without any expectation in return. You are not controlled by ego or the selfish need to make yourself feel better and more powerful, because these things no longer exist, because you killed them in you.

THE KNOWN, THE UNKNOWN AND THE UNKNOWABLE

- The 'known' are things that you have learnt.

- The 'unknown' are things that you can learn.

- The 'unknowable' are things that you'll never know or understand, until they appear 'to you, through you'.

As an example, at one point in time, people believed the Earth was flat, and those that challenged that idea were executed. We now know the Earth is a sphere, and that belief has become acceptable globally. And just like that, there are things about death that you are not expected to know or understand until it's your time. In the meantime, these are some thoughts on death for you to sit with, get comfortable with and be prepared for, because inevitably we are all going to die one day.

THE GAME OF DEATH

You can start to see how death envelops life, and life envelops death, in everyday life. The moment something dies, something else is born. After all, even Newton knew the life and death cycle on an energetic level when he said:

> 'Energy cannot be created or destroyed,
> It just changes from one form to another.'

And just like that… the moment you decided to take up martial arts, you decided to kill something in you, didn't you? Some kind of trauma caused by bullying, a loss of a loved one, lack of self-worth/self-confidence, build-up of stress, etc.

The moment you step through the door of your dojo, you're killing your ego and leaving it outside, otherwise you wouldn't learn anything because your teacup would be too full – and your ego already knows everything, right?

The moment you step into your first sparring match, you're killing all your demons and inner voices that are scared of getting punched in the face, scared of losing, aren't you?

Something is dying all the time, so you can live. That is…

> 'The Game of Death'.

What if you could kill all the things that stand in your way in daily life, so you could get out of your own way and start to move forward and really live and experience life to its truest potential?

I like to say:

> 'To understand death is to understand life.
> To accept death is to accept life.
> Only then you understand:
> Death gives life.'

In Bruce Lee's own words:

> 'Don't neglect life by worrying about death. I don't know what is the meaning of death, but I am not afraid to die… and I go on, non-stop, going forward [with life]. Even though, I, Bruce Lee, may die some day without fulfilling all of my ambitions, I will have no regrets.'

So, stop worrying about dying, and start playing 'The Game of Death' so you can start living.

FULL OF EMPTINESS

THE TRUE MEANING OF A BLACK BELT

MYTHS AND ANCESTRAL SECRETS OF THE BLACK BELT

When people think of a Black Belt, there are two main trails of thought. One is enveloped in *Mystique,* full of charisma, glamour, romance, mystery, fascination, magic, charm, appeal, allure and awe… and the other shrouded in *Scepticism,* filled with doubt, distrust, suspicion, disbelief and pessimism.

I'm going to bust the Black Belt myths and reveal the ancestral secrets of the true meaning of the Black Belt. Here goes…

THE BIRTH OF THE BLACK BELT

In Judo, Black Belts have been around since the mid-1880s. They were first issued by Jigaro Kano (founder of Judo) as a visual tool to distinguish students' skill levels from one another so he could teach them accordingly. However, the concept of a Black Belt was not handed down from ancient martial arts masters, secret scrolls or ancient buried manuscripts – rather un-glamorously, Jigaro got the idea from a Japanese public school swimming programme.

In 1907, Jigaro introduced the *Judogi* (uniform) in two colours, white for the beginners known as *Mudansha* and black for the experts known as *Yudansha.* The Judogi's white colour represents simplicity, purity, and emptiness at the beginning of the martial journey, eventually filled with knowledge, represented by black.

The sweat, blood and tears of sacrifice and perseverance towards self-mastery was later represented by Black Belts with red stripes, today replaced with solid red belts predominantly awarded as honorary belts to Judo Masters (9th Dan+), introduced by Jigaro in the 1930s. In 1935, Mikonosuke Kawaishi introduced additional colours as a way to motivate his students further towards greater achievement. The colour belt system was adopted by other Japanese martial arts systems such as Karate and Jiu Jitsu, and this idea slowly spread across other martial art disciplines across the globe to where we are now.

ORIGINS OF THE BLACK BELT

Traditionally, martial arts were created to serve and protect families/ clans in more barbaric times. Hence traditional martial arts schools were based on family/clan warfare secrets. These secrets were not allowed to be shared outside of the dojo or the master's home. The survival of the family/clan was dependent on the element of mystery and fear of their deadly secret techniques, to fend off potential threats, and of course the ability to fight effectively when it came down to it.

Prospective students who wished to join a martial arts school would be carefully screened and assessed before being accepted into the family/clan. As part of their initiation ceremony, they would be given the family uniform and a white belt as a means of formal acceptance into the family/clan and representing their submission to their teacher's commands.

Over time, the student would be assessed for progression through:

- Cultivating skills and knowledge,

- Growth and proficiency,

- Hard work and perseverance,

- Justice and fairness,

- Courage and indomitable spirit,

- Mercy and forgiveness,

- Politeness and respect,

- Honesty and sincerity,

- Honour and integrity,

- Loyalty and dedication,

- Character and self-control, and

- Self-mastery,

…and promoted to a belt/sash representing a higher rank, eventually reaching *Cho-dan* (First Degree Black Belt) and beyond.

In Japan, sensei means:

> 'One born before or twice born.'

On a physical level, this implies age and experience, and on the spiritual level, the original two Japanese characters reveal:

> 'One who has been before,' or, 'Filled with an ancestral spirit.'

A Grand Master or Founder is known as a *Sijo* or *Soke* – a declaration of the 'Head of the Family/Clan' and their corresponding martial art and warfare secrets. The head of the family was given supreme respect and obedience and treated on par with God, and when a new student joined a school, they were taught to yield the highest honour, respect and obedience to the head of their martial family.

Any violation of this, with or without the instructor present, at the dojo or master's home was severely frowned upon and often hindered the progress of the student's training and rank.

Figure 3: Japanese character for 'Cho-dan'

Cho-dan means 'First Degree Black Belt'. It is made up of two symbols:

- A knife 刀

- And clothing 衣

This represents how when making a garment, you must first cut the fabric. The Cho-dan rank of Black Belt therefore does not represent mastery, but rather the beginning of creating the martial artist.

A PUNCH IS JUST A PUNCH

Learning martial arts is like painting. In the beginning, a student has to learn how to:

- Hold a paintbrush.

- Apply paint to the paintbrush.

- Apply paint from the paintbrush onto the canvas.

- Create different effects using the paint.

Up until the Black Belt, a student is merely learning how to use his tools… their paintbrush, paint and canvas.

Only after this time does a student really start to delve into their 'personal artistic expression' of what kind of art they are going to create.

Over time, the student gets better and better at painting, to the point they no longer think about how to use their tools… that happens automatically. What they do with them then becomes their post Cho-dan experience towards their true mastery and understanding, by actually revealing who they really are through their own true personal expression.

I like to say:

> 'Before enlightenment, a punch is just a punch.
> During enlightenment, a punch is no longer a punch.
> After enlightenment, a punch is just a punch.'

WHAT ARE BELTS GOOD FOR?

Bruce Lee famously said:

> 'Belts are only good for holding up your pants.'

When Bruce said this, there was a big misconception and uproar that he was denigrating other martial arts, and that he believed the belt system had no value. That couldn't be further from the truth.

What Bruce was getting at was that the West had manipulated the belt system as a means to lure people into Black Belt programmes, promising them all the glory and honour of becoming a martial artist by sharing ancient secrets, though compromising honesty and integrity for maximising student numbers for commercial gain, churning out Black Belts that couldn't hold their own when it came to a real fight. These martial arts schools are often referred to as McDojos, and they have been mostly responsible for the Black Belt scepticism that exists today.

The expectation today is that if someone is putting effort, time and money into their training, then they'll earn their belt. Back in the old days, only the deepest level of knowledge and understanding, and the ability to demonstrate that without help was recognised as worthy of promotion to a higher belt/sash/rank.

Hence, for some, their Black Belt is literally only good for holding up their pants, because it represents nothing in terms of their ability to stand up for themselves, let alone others.

WHEN A BLACK BELT IS NO LONGER A BLACK BELT

In the beginning, a student sees a Black Belt as:

- The highest level of martial artistry.

- An aspirational goal.

- A role model and teacher.

During your journey towards achieving a Black Belt, there is blood, sweat, tears and laughter through the highs and the lows, where:

- Your skill is tested.

- Your fitness is tested.

- Your willpower is tested.

- Your fear is tested.

- Your character is tested.

- Your maturity is tested.

- Your perseverance is tested.

- Your emotional resilience is tested.

- Your self-discipline is tested.

- Your fighting spirit is tested.

The biggest misconception of a Black Belt is that it is something you earn – WRONG!!!

A Black Belt is something you BECOME.

When you are honoured with a Black Belt, nothing changes, yet everything changes. People look up to you, and you have a massive responsibility to:

- Serve and protect your family/clan with valour and grace.

- Uphold the values and virtues of your family/clan.

- Maintain honour and integrity.

- Be a leader with humility and humbleness, and lead by example.

- Always extend politeness and respect.

- Act consciously in all areas of your life.

- Continue to sharpen your sword of Self Mastery.

- Transcend your learnings from the dojo to everyday life.

And once you have discovered your gift, you have an obligation to give it away selflessly.

If you abuse that power, you'll tarnish all that the Black Belt stands for, and you'll no longer represent a true Black Belt, or an honest martial artist, for that matter.

In Judo, the Black Belt is the beginning of the Mastery (Red Belt) journey, which is the honorary path, not the familiar McDojo monthly awards party train.

FULL OF EMPTINESS

A Black Belt honours, preserves and promotes the roots of their ancestral teachings. They serve and protect their family/clan against threats, and this IS a massive social and leadership responsibility. During a Black Belt ritual, a Wu Dang Tai Chi Grand Master once said to his student:

'Now you are a disciple.
This is your home.
Your business is our business, and ours is yours.
Do you understand?'

And as we sharpen our sword of consciousness using the whetstone of Self Mastery inspired by martial arts to discover who we really are, we start to realise it was never about 'I'. It was always about nurturing and protecting 'US' and our greatest matriarch… Mother Earth.

A Zen Master once said:

'Knowledge is learning something every day.
Wisdom is letting go of something every day.'

A student full of Black Belt knowledge will eventually realise in order to continue on their path of Mastery, they must 'empty their mind' and leave everything they've learnt behind – i.e. become a White Belt again, so they are liberated to walk on!

A Black Belt is a mindset which is 'full of emptiness'.

TAKE ACTION AND MASTER YOUR LIFE

BLACK BELT MINDSET

1. **Decide** what well-formed outcome you want to Master in Your Life.

2. Develop a **strategy and plan** to Attain Your Mastery.

3. Learn a **Black Belt mindset,** that no matter what, You Will Succeed in achieving your well-formed outcome.

4. **Take massive action** to Get Massive Results, to Get Massive Belief in yourself. And every step of the way, say to yourself, "I GOT THIS!"

SWORD OF CONSCIOUSNESS

TRANSCENDING MARTIAL ARTS

SHARPENING YOUR SWORD

A martial artist cultivates his **body as a weapon**, so when they or a loved one is put in harm's way, they have the combative tools to incapacitate the aggressor as quickly as possible.

A martial artist cultivates his **mind as a weapon,** so when they or a loved one is put in harm's way, they have the calmness, control and calibration to find a way not to fight and resolve the situation with mental and emotional intelligence.

A martial artist cultivates his **spirit as a weapon,** so when they or a loved one is put in harm's way, they have the compassion and kindness to connect to the other person's heart and soul, through their divine intelligence.

A martial artist is someone who invests extensive time, energy and resources to sharpen their Sword of Consciousness, to reveal his true power and authentic highest self over a prolonged period of time.

But few people, let alone martial artists, truly recognise the immense power they possess.

WIELDING YOUR SWORD

Your thoughts, words and actions can be like a sharp sword being wielded recklessly. As they say, there are five things you cannot take back:

- A stone after it is thrown.

- A word once it is spoken.

- An occasion once it is missed.

- An action once it is done.

- Time once it has passed.

We are powerful beyond our greatest beliefs, and as Confucius said:

> 'You will never know how sharp a sword is,
> Until it is drawn from its sheath.'

But little do we realise how dangerous our tamest and most innocent of thoughts, words and actions can be, often causing the gravest harm unknowingly.

KNOWLEDGE IS POWER

Bruce Lee said:

> 'If knowledge is power,
> Then do not give it away indiscriminately.'

A martial arts teacher has a huge responsibility to ensure they carefully screen their prospective students to ensure they are sound of mind and character and capable of handling the burden of responsibility that comes with unleashing the power within, so they do not abuse and pervert it towards their own selfish needs to the detriment of others and their environment.

When the student learns deadly techniques that can injure, maim, disable and potentially kill someone, they have the highest responsibility to use those weapons with absolute discretion. This is a skill that can only be cultivated through honing one's consciousness with the whetstone of Self-Mastery.

A Pirelli advert from 2005 featuring world champion sprinter, Carl Lewis, in a race ready crouch position wearing bright red stilettos with the following slogan sums this up nicely,

'Power is nothing without control.'

BLUNTING OUR SWORDS

If you have ever learnt how to use different types of swords to cut objects, one of the things you will have discovered is that each type of sword has a unique sweet spot.

If you use your sword incorrectly, it will not cut as smoothly and cleanly as it could. Moreover, you could jam your sword in the object you are trying to cut, blunting your sword over time.

Likewise, our thoughts, words and actions can be like careless blows of a sword, slowly blunting our consciousness… dumbing us down over time when used incorrectly.

CUTTING KARMA

Therefore, our daily conscious actions either sharpen our sword or blunt it.

To sharpen our sword, we must understand the consequences of our actions, and equally as important, our inactions. I like to say:

'I am what I do, and
I am what I do not do.'

When you perform negative actions/inactions, then you create karmic debt, i.e. you owe someone something.

When you perform positive actions/inactions with expectation, then you create karmic credit, i.e. someone owes you something in return.

Both karmic debt and karmic credit will eventually burden your consciousness. Your 'conscience' is your reminder that there is karmic debt or credit that needs to be settled, and it often makes you feel like you're carrying a heavy weight on your shoulders and prevents you from living your life to its truest and truthful potential.

When you refrain from negative actions or perform positive actions without expectation, then you do not create any karma. When you correct your ill actions/inactions through thanks, forgiveness and love, then you can pay off karmic debt or settle any karmic credit.

That is, you can cut, dissolve and neutralise all karma and reach the zero point... the point of buoyancy and weightlessness where your conscience and consciousness have been cut free by your Sword of Consciousness, liberated to fly free.

The Bhagavad Gita states:

> 'A man who sees action in inaction,
> And inaction in action,
> Has understanding among men,
> And discipline in all actions he performs.'

THE SEVEN GENERATION RULE

We believe our ancestors to have been nomadic hunter-gatherers. Their tribes traversed the plains for survival, following food and water throughout the changing seasons, harsh cold winters and scorching hot summers.

When the Native Americans found a potential new site for a settlement that would provide their tribe with the food and water they needed, the chief would exercise 'The Seven Generation Rule,' a test which posed seven powerful questions:

1. Would our actions/inactions be of detriment to our generation?

2. Would our actions/inactions be of detriment to our children's generation?

3. Would our actions/inactions be of detriment to our grandchildren's generation?

4. Would our actions/inactions be of detriment to our great-grandchildren's generation?

5. Would our actions/inactions be of detriment to our great-great-grandchildren's generation?

6. Would our actions/inactions be of detriment to our great-great-great-grandchildren's generation?

7. Would our actions/inactions be of detriment to our great-great great-great-grandchildren's generation?

If any generation was affected negatively by the action/inaction in question, then they simply would not do that thing and look for an alternative solution. This allowed the Native Americans to not only preserve quality of life for the next seven generations, but also leave Mother Earth in a better position than when they arrived.

For everything they cut down, they would re-sow. For everything they hunted, they would hunt no more than needed. For all the water they used, they would ensure it did not affect other life dependent on that water source.

A RUSTY SWORD

There are four stages of learning:

1. **Unconscious Incompetence** – When you do not know you are not very good at something.

2. **Conscious Incompetence** – When you do know you are not very good at something and are working on getting better at it.

3. **Conscious Competence** – When you know you are getting good at something and continue to work on it.

4. **Unconscious Competence** – When you do not know you are really good at something because you've been doing it for so long, it becomes second nature.

Across the world, we have slowly moved away from the Unconscious Competence of the conscious nomadic tribal way of life and bought into utilitarian city life. This has shifted the power and responsibility for hunting and gathering of food and water (amongst other modern-day creature comforts and luxuries) to the utility providers, who produce and supply us with our food, drink, medicine, clothing, housing, heating, communication, transport, education, information and entertainment.

At first, the population had a say in how the utility companies conducted themselves, as we had workers' unions that had a voice to complain and strike if they disagreed with their company's unethical practices or mistreatment of their employees. Over time, we saw the unions shut down, muting the voices of the population, which slowly withdrew our attention from the way the utility companies conducted their business.

The privatisation and globalisation of our utility companies further shifted their mindsets to economic, business-focussed ones, with the companies using advancements in engineering and technology to produce more goods and services for cheaper. An obsession with profits, further shifting their attention away from making conscious decisions concerning the people and the planet, has become widespread.

As consumers got used to the daily creature comforts and luxuries on offer in greater quantities for cheaper, we slowly forgot the ill effects our consumption has had. We have forgotten that what we consume has an effect on the people, all sentient beings and the planet.

What started out as a positive way to give our populous the creature comforts and luxuries we desired accidentally became damaging to the people and environment. You could say we accidentally became Unconsciously Incompetent at acting consciously, like a neglected sword becomes rusty.

RESTORING OUR SWORD

We can restore our sword from its neglect by taking small, conscious, effortless steps with love as a collective human race on our home, Mother Earth.

We just need to start asking the questions our nomadic tribal ancestors asked before they took action/inaction, such as:

1. Are my actions/inactions causing suffering to myself, other sentient beings and/or Mother Earth?

2. Are my resources sourced and produced consciously? (Food, drink, medicine, clothing, housing, heating, communication, transport, education, information, and entertainment).

3. If you answer NOT SURE or NO to questions #1
   and/or #2:

   - Take responsibility for doing your own research
     to obtain the facts.

   - Ask yourself, do I really need this?

   - And if so, what other conscious sources
     can I get my resources from instead?

4. Then simply change your supplier(s)/resource and/or
   reduce/eliminate the amount of that resource you use.

Already we are seeing utility companies changing the way they
provide our resources to become more ethical, because if there's
enough demand, they will eventually supply it – it's in their best
interest, as it is in ours. It's a win-win situation!

If it costs more, but you really want to make a positive change
to living consciously for everyone and the environment, then pay
more for it now until it gets cheaper; as more people switch over,
production costs will reduce over time.

Simply by being conscious of what we are eating, drinking, healing and
medicating with, purchasing, watching, listening, reading, connecting
to, conversing with and loving… can have a massive positive effect
on ourselves, other sentient beings and Mother Earth.

Bandamanna Saga, a wise man, once said:

> 'When truth and fairness are different from what is law,
>   Better it is to follow truth and fairness.'

THE CONSCIOUS WARRIOR

A Greek proverb says:

> 'A society grows great when old men plant trees,
> Whose shade they know they shall never sit in.'

A true martial artist knows:

> 'It takes great courage to pick up a sword.
> It takes greater courage not to use it.'
> – Being Caballero

It's time to pick up your Sword of Consciousness and use it wisely with compassion and kindness to sow those trees whose shade we will never know.

It is not to hurt anyone, but to heal yourself, other sentient beings and Mother Earth by changing your conscious lifestyle behaviours. To neutralise not only your carbon footprint, but your karmic footprint as well.

It is about taking your knowledge and power back and using it responsibly with absolute discrimination towards your Original Truth.

The battle for humanity and Mother Earth is not one which can be fought, it is one which can literally be taught and practised by sharpening your Sword of Consciousness with the whetstone of Self Mastery. Remember…

> 'There's a battle going on.
> Keep your eyes open,
> And your sword sharp.'

TAKE ACTION AND MASTER YOUR LIFE

THREE SWORDS OF TRUTH

In ancient Greece, Socrates was visited by an acquaintance. Eager to share some juicy gossip, the man asked if Socrates would like to know the story he'd just heard about a friend of theirs. Socrates replied that before the man spoke, he needed to pass the 'Three Swords of Truth' test.

Socrates asked, "Have you made absolutely sure that what you are about to say is true?"

The man shook his head. "No, I actually just heard about it, and…"

Socrates cut him off. "You don't know for certain that it is true, then. Is what you want to say something good or kind?"

Again, the man shook his head. "No! Actually, just the opposite. You see…"

Socrates lifted his hand to stop the man speaking. "So you are not certain that what you want to say is true, and it isn't good or kind."

Lastly, Socrates asked, "Is this information useful or necessary to me?"

A little defeated, the man replied, "No, not really."

"Well, then," Socrates said, turning on his heel. "If what you want to say is neither true, nor good or kind, nor useful or necessary, please don't say anything at all."

When thinking, speaking or acting, use Socrates' 'Three Swords of Truth':

     1. Sword of Truth: Is it true?
     2. Sword of Goodness: Is it good?
     3. Sword of Usefulness: Is it useful?

THE HAPPINESS HOAX

IT'S NOT ALL ABOUT BEING HAPPY

TRAIN HARD, FIGHT EASY

As martial artists, we train hard so when push comes to shove and we have to fight for a just cause, we can fight confidently with relative ease and graceful, lightning-fast movements to incapacitate our foes.

To get to that level, we endure hours of hard training with sweat, blood and tears. We experience black eyes, split lips, black and blue bruises, not to mention the bruising of our egos. We put ourselves in difficult positions so we can face and conquer our innermost demons—remember the first time you stepped up to spar and felt the butterflies in your belly?

None of this is to attain happiness but rather, like a samurai sword, which is:

- Heated to white-hot temperatures,

- Beaten repetitively,

- Folded a hundred times,

- Thrown into a cold-water trough to harden, and

- Rubbed abrasively by a whetstone.

We train so we can sharpen our swords, be better versions of ourselves, and reveal a work of art inside that rough block of steel.

STATE OF AFFAIRS

Quite often we hear people say things like:

- "I would be happy if…" or

- "I would be happy when…"

Happiness is not a condition or a destination.

Happiness is in fact a **state.**

Like a light, you can turn happiness ON and OFF with a flick of a switch.

We can all relate to the moment when you listen to a song which reminds you of a happy time in your life and all of a sudden all your worries melt away into a momentary state of happiness. On the flip side, when you listen to a sad song, it often makes you feel unhappy and gloomy.

AS LONG AS YOU ARE HAPPY

We live in a world where our daily mantra is slowly becoming, "As long as you are happy," condoning actions that put you in a temporary state of happiness.

What this does not take into account is sometimes your happiness comes at the cost of someone else's. You cannot build your own happiness on the foundation of somebody else's misery. That has a karmic footprint which comes with consequence (see previous chapter for more information on this topic).

Martial arts teach us to take responsibility for and ownership of our actions. For example, when a beginner spars against an advanced student for the first time, most advanced students have an innate tendency to 'take it easy' and ease the beginner into the flow, foregoing their egos, coaching them with a sense of care, knowing full well the damage they could inflict if they really wanted to.

Likewise, in everyday life, if we recognise the power of our choices and actions in the same way, with care, responsibility and ownership, we start to realise:

- We don't act towards our own happiness,

- Neither do we act towards others' happiness, but in fact

- We act towards **doing what's right** when we become consciously awake.

YOU CHOSE THIS LIFE

Indigenous cultures all over the world share a common belief that we choose our own parents and life experiences so they will help us reveal who we really are in this lifetime.

Bruce Lee called this self-realisation. I call it Self Mastery.

That is, the process of:

- Accepting everything that happens in your life is by your choice,

- When you start to do that, you can start to see the lesson in each life experience,

- Which helps to reveal a little bit more of who you really are,

...until one day, like the samurai sword, you reveal a powerful piece of beautiful artwork.

OUR TEACHERS

Bruce Lee stated:

'Life itself is your teacher,
And you're in a constant state of learning.'

Our teachers come in two forms, that is:

- **Inspiration,** and

- **Suffering.**

People seldom take heed of the inspirational way of learning/self-realisation due to comfort and/or complacency, so life ends up throwing a curve ball of whoop-ass suffering so they have to learn the hard way.

It is only when the suffering becomes unbearable that people retreat and go inwards to 'find themselves' and seek reasons why these things are happening to them.

GOOD VIBRATIONS

Absolutely everything in the universe as we know it is just a mere vibration. Let me explain…

At the most fundamental level of physics, there are three states: solids, liquids and gases. They all consist of molecules, which are a collection of atoms. Atoms are made up of electrons which orbit a nucleus, which comprises of neutrons and protons. The relative distance between the nucleus and the orbiting electrons is the same as the Earth to its moon. In between, there is just a vastness of empty space. They are held together by invisible vibratory forces, often referred to as 'energy'. Therefore, we are made up of intrinsic vibrational energy.

As human beings, we have the ability to detect vibratory energy, and often people will say they get good or bad vibes about things. This is called intuition… a knowing.

The ancient scripture the Bhagavad Gita describes the universe as being made up of three subtle vibratory energies:

- **Tama** – the lowest vibratory energy,
  which relates to our ignorance,

- **Raja** – the medium vibratory energy,
  which relates to our actions and passion

- **Sattva** – the highest vibratory energy,
  which relates to spiritual purity,
  purpose and higher wisdom.

Quite often we hear people say, 'Follow your passion and you will be happy.' Again, this couldn't be further from the Original Truth. I like to say:

'Passion is not your path,
Your path is your purpose.'

This is known as your *Dharma*.

Cultivating your vibration to a higher state takes *Sadhana,* that is sitting in deep meditation, with study, patience, concentration and surrender.

MOVING MEDITATION

Martial arts are merely Moving Meditations to cultivate your Self Mastery, slowly revealing who you are:

- Beyond body.

- Beyond mind.

- Beyond emotion.

- Beyond soul.

When your thoughts and self slip away, you start moving towards your true essence.

Martial arts are already doing this, through helping you to understand:

- Mastery of your body,

- Mastery of your mind,

- Mastery of your emotions, and

- Mastery of your fighting spirit.

HAPPY OR UNHAPPY

Life isn't about being happy or unhappy. It is about revealing who you really are at your true highest vibrational self. Everything in between is a process of removing the veil of illusion, or *maya* in Sanskrit. In Sikhi, your true authentic highest self is called *Sat Naam,* i.e. your true name, your true identity, your Original Truth.

When you connect with your Original Truth, you self-realise and you will experience *Ananda,* i.e. bliss. This is not happiness, it is not a temporary state, it is a place of eternal joy. People who have experienced this bliss often refer to it as **Love** (not in the Valentine's sense), being:

- A knowing of the unknowing, not just a blind belief.

- A contentment, not just a reconciliation.

- A certainty, not just speculation.

- A centredness, not just balance.

- A weightlessness, not just a fleeting feeling of lightness.

- A natural flow, not just an idea of moving towards your success.

- Absolute love, compassion and kindness.

At the highest level, martial arts are about love. We only ever fight in the name of love. To protect the ones we love and the things we love, be that ourselves, our loved ones, our belongings or even our ego (that we are trying to shed, whether you realise that or not).

You only realise that when you have the martial skills to seriously hurt someone, but instead you use your gifts to heal them instead. That is the start of your higher expression of the true self.

Thich Nhat Hanh beautifully summed this up when he said:

'Finding truth is not the same as finding happiness.
You aspire to see the truth.
But once you have seen it,
You cannot avoid suffering.
Otherwise you have seen nothing at all.'

TAKE ACTION AND MASTER YOUR LIFE

CHIN UP

Our physiology can change our emotional state.

When we droop our shoulders, drop our heads and stare towards the ground, hunching our backs, we start to sense a feeling of sadness. When we lift our chins and chests, straighten our backs, stand upright and look up, we start to sense a feeling of confidence and happiness. And just like that, we can switch from unhappy to happy.

To practise managing your emotional state, the next time you walk up the street, look up and count the number of chimneys on your way to work, home, or wherever you're going.

As they say, chin up.

SHAMAH

(PRONOUNCED: SHUM-AH)
THE ART OF FORGIVENESS

DEALING WITH THE AFTERTASTE OF A FIGHT

Martial arts usually focus on how to avoid getting into a fight, and when there is no other choice but to fight for a 'just' cause, you should incapacitate your opponent(s) as swiftly and gracefully as possible using reasonable force. Seldom do we focus on the bitter aftertaste left behind after a fight and how to dissolve that. Let's delve deeper into this...

WHY PEOPLE FIGHT

People fight for many reasons, such as when they:

1. Get offended,

2. Feel threatened,

3. Feel scared,

4. Are treated badly,

5. Have had something stolen from them,

6. Are under extreme pressure,

7. Feel disrespected,

8. Experience injustice,

9. Have their values and beliefs violated,

10. Have a bias towards a specific tribe,

...to name but a few.

All these boil down to one root cause…
LOVE! That's right – LOVE! It is the love for:

- **Something,** e.g. car, house or other material object.

- **Someone,** e.g. your family, friends and tribe.

- **Beliefs,** e.g. rules, rights and religion.

- **Yourself,** e.g. your ego identity.

THE AFTERTASTE

When people fight, they are usually left with a bitter aftertaste of shame and/or guilt (which can also be expressed by other negative emotions such as anger, hatred and dejection), whether directly from their actions/inactions imposed on them unjustly as a consequence of someone else's actions/inactions.

Shame often signifies violation of cultural or social values, while feelings of guilt arise from violation of one's own internal values and beliefs.

Shame and guilt are a sign of incongruence between your truth and your, or someone else's, actions/inactions, alerted by your conscience as an inner distress and discomfort.

Shame and guilt play negative tricks on your mind and emotions, and can lead to illness of the body, until you eventually muster the courage to resolve the matter once you have the resources to deal with it.

FISTICUFFS

Just to set the record straight, not all fights leave a bitter aftertaste of shame and guilt.

The Irish Travellers are famous for their fisticuffs, that is going 'toe-to-toe' to resolve a dispute. Once the fight is over, the two parties shake hands in a gentlemanly manner, hug it out, and the issue is forgiven on both sides and put to rest forever, leaving a sweet taste of contentment and humility.

No bystanders jump in, and there is a code-of-conduct such as no throws, eye-gouging or hair-pulling, and each fighter has a 'fair play man' who acts as a referee to make sure it's a clean fight.

Often misconceived as barbaric bare-knuckled fighting, this is in fact fighting with honour and pride. This is an original form of Irish martial arts called Dornalaiocht, which we now know as modern boxing (also referred to as the Irish stand down, bare-knuckle, prize-fighting, pugilism, toe-to-toe, fist fight or fisticuffs).

This chapter, however, focuses on fights where a dispute is left unresolved leaving a sense of shame and/or guilt.

WHAT IS SHAMAH?

Shamah (pronounced shum-ah) is a Sanskrit word that means 'forgiveness'.

The word 'shame' has very similar phonetic roots, originally believed to have been derived from the Old English word hama, meaning a veil or covering that one wears to signal penitence.

Shamah, therefore, is the un-veiling of the covering, the lifting and release of the shame and guilt, with a surrender to your vulnerability while being submerged in humility – which is easier said than done.

Shamah therefore requires immense **mental, emotional and spiritual mastery,** so one can **truly forgive from the heart and soul** by removing their ego defence.

FORGET ME NOT

Most people have heard the saying: 'Forgive and forget.'

The truth of the matter is the unconscious mind never forgets anything… EVER! It is an infinite store of information (whether you have the skill to recall that information is a different matter).

Therefore, true forgiveness remembers everything.
So why would you…

> Choose to live in the past,
> And reflect that onto your future,
> To re-create past experiences,
> Which no longer serve you in the present.

…it's a vicious circle!

Rather, forgiveness focuses on accepting and embracing the past and making peace with it, living in the present the best you can, so you can create new fond memories right now, to shape a better and brighter future.

FACING DEATH

Picture yourself at a funeral, staring at the coffin about to be reeled into the cremator or lowered in the ground. You have a lasting reminder that this is the final farewell. You have a sudden realisation that we are all heading in the same direction, and that our existence on Mother Earth is merely a temporary one. You are left with a stark realisation that…

Life is too short.

You have a moment of clarity when you realise all the fighting and drama is meaningless and feeble, and you experience an overwhelming sense of humility and insignificance in the face of death, and an appreciation for the life you still have.

The question is… What are you going to do with all this new-found wisdom?

MISO NO KORO

To truly practise the art of Shamah, you have to be like the 'Moon in the Lake'.

Picture a moon glistening in a tranquil lake. Notice how the lake does not attach itself to the moon, though it is a direct reflection of all the moon's heavenly glory.

To see the true reflection of the moon clearly, the lake has to become totally calm and still.

Remember: **recollection, anticipation and wants** are all **sources of attachment,** which cause ripples in the lake, obscuring the reflection of the moon. We have heard it all before – he did this, she did that; he said this, she said that; I should've done this, I could've done that; and so on.

Only when you practise the art of *Miso no Koro* – stilling your mind like water – do you become aware of your sources of attachment and become able to work on detaching from them.

Only then will you notice your true shine is a reflection of all the light outside of you, as well as all the light inside of you.

Only then will you start to notice the water has been moving all the time, and you are able to flow with it.

KARMIC FLAVOURS

Karma comes in three flavours:

1. **Karmic Debt:** This is when you do something untoward to someone and you create a negative karma – a debt you have to pay back to that person.

2. **Karmic Credit:** This is when you do something nice for someone and you expect something in return, creating a positive karma – a credit the other person has to pay back to you in some way, shape or form.

3. **Zero Point:** This is when you do something kind and compassionate for someone without any expectations. This is pure selfless servitude, called *Seva* in Guru Granth Sahib Ji, the sacred scriptures of the Sikhs.

True Shamah sits peacefully at the Zero Point, not creating any karma. Wayne Dyer summed this up beautifully when he said:

'How people treat you is their karma.
How you react is yours.'

KENSHŌ

Indigenous tribes and ancient cultures believe that we choose the life experiences we have in this lifetime so we can evolve spiritually to reveal who we really are, our Original Truth, and return 'home'.

Ancient wisdom teaches us that anyone who inspires us or causes us suffering to reveal who we really are is a **life teacher** (or 'agent of the universe') sent especially to serve us. We therefore have an obligation and responsibility to seek the lesson in that experience so we can ascend.

The Japanese call this *Kenshō* – *ken* means 'seeing', *shō* means 'nature, essence'. It is usually translated as 'seeing one's essential nature', that is, our Buddha-nature. Kenshō is an initial insight or awakening, not necessarily full Buddhahood.

If we miss or ignore the teaching, then life will repeat the lesson with increasing severity until you actually have no choice to but to face yourself.

The hardest thing to do is to **thank your life teachers** for serving you through inspiration and, in particular, suffering.

WHAT IS THE COLOUR OF THE WIND?

What did you experience momentarily when you read…
What is the colour of the wind?

…An emptiness drifting in the wind, perhaps.

This Zen Koan helps us to experience emptiness or no-thingness, if you may. The wind signifies thoughts drifting away, creating a sense of non-attachment, non-being, no-thingness, or *Mu* in Japanese.

Martial arts teach us to cultivate a state of Mu so we can respond intelligently to whatever strike comes our way. For when we become attached to a thought such as, 'if this happens, then I will do this, that, and the other,' that is usually when we get punched in the face. Mike Tyson famously said:

> 'Everyone's got a plan,
> Until they get punched in the face.'

Similarly, when we fight, we get attached to the thoughts, emotions and feelings associated with the fight, rather than seek freedom from something which is no longer really happening.

IT'S ALL A GAME

Like in a game of Monopoly (or any other board game for that matter), in the end… everything goes back in the box (just like you will at your funeral).

When you understand this, you will start to understand true freedom.

So, stop fussing over petty things and start enjoying playing the game – while it lasts.

THE THREE EGO WEAPONS

As part of the 'human condition', we all suffer from
The Three Ego Weapons, which are:

  1. Fear and anxiety.

  2. Separation and animosity.

  3. Shame and guilt.

MIND THE GAP

When we fight and a bad aftertaste is left behind, we create a gap
between the people and tribes involved in the conflict. Where there
is a gap, it fills with one or more of **The Three Ego Weapons.**
The wider the gap, the greater the damage caused by The Three
Ego Weapons.

To close the gap, you have to decide:

  1. Whether it is worth **reconnecting with love;** or

  2. Whether this relationship has served you,
     and you are free to **walk on.**

As they say on the London Underground:

  'Mind the gap.'

CHILD'S PLAY

Picture two young siblings playing with a toy, and all of a sudden they start fighting over the toy. Moments later, they will be back to playing with one another as if nothing ever happened. They don't hold a grudge in their hearts; rather, they dissolve all the negative emotions and carry on playing because the negativity no longer serves them and it is simply more enjoyable and effortless to let it go.

We can learn a lot from children. We have simply forgotten the way to **love playfully** due to social conditioning and conformance, and rigidity in education and corporate life, that has beaten the 'child's play' out of us. Children, as vulnerable as they are, have an amazing innate ability to forgive, because they operate from a place of pure innocence and egolessness, unconditional love and sheer joy of playfulness. They naturally exist in a state of Shamah.

> Shamah is courage and strength whilst sitting in your vulnerability.
>
> Shamah is quietening of the ego and submerging yourself in humility.
>
> Shamah is liberating yourself from other people's karmic actions/inactions.
>
> Shamah is responding intelligently with kindness, compassion and love.
>
> Shamah is connecting with our inner-child's innocence, unconditional love, joy and playfulness.
>
> Shamah is ultimately – Self Mastery.

As Brene Brown, in a TED Talk on vulnerability, put it:

> 'Empathy is the antidote to shame and kills the secrecy, silence and judgment.
>
> You can stand outside the arena and feel invincible and achieve nothing, or you can step into the arena of vulnerability and grow, regardless of whether you fail or succeed.'

And so it happens to be...

If the reason people **START** fighting is **FOR LOVE,**
Then the reason people **STOP** fighting is **THROUGH LOVE.**

TAKE ACTION AND MASTER YOUR LIFE

THE ART OF FORGIVENESS

To practise the Art of Forgiveness:

1. Choose someone/something you want to forgive.

2. Still the mind so you can start to think and see clearly.

3. Become aware of your attachments to them/that thing.

4. List your vulnerabilities around this space.

5. List what your ego is saying.

6. List all the karmic actions/inactions/trespasses done unto you/others.

Now...

1. See the life lesson in that, and embrace that wholly.

2. Sit in your vulnerabilities and make yourself comfortable, finding strength in doing so.

3. Allow your ego to quiet down, and submerge yourself in humility, repeating "there is no I".

4. Separate and release their actions/inactions as their own (not yours).

5. Send them kindness, compassion and love.

6. Decide how you're going to close the gap.

7. Then take the appropriate action/inaction to close the gap.

8. And most of all, expect nothing in return and do it with pure intent, joy, playfulness, and most importantly, love.

ULTIMATE POTENTIAL

LIVING YOUR BEST LIFE

CREATING THE ULTIMATE LIFE USING MARTIAL ART PRINCIPLES

The yin and yang symbol is synonymous with martial arts, and is often used in martial art school logos.

The true meaning of the yin and yang actually comes from Chinese philosophy and is an integral part of Taoism, Ch'an (Zen) Buddhism and the *I Ching*. The philosophy behind yin and yang describes the **natural order of the universe.**

It is a common misconception in the Western world that yin and yang represent a dualistic view of the world, such as:

- Black and white.

- Good and bad.

- Light and dark.

- Gentleness and firmness.

- Hot and cold.

- Life and death.

- Male and female.

- Active and passive.

- Strength and weakness.

- Cause and effect.

- Fire and water.

- Sun and moon.

However, yin and yang actually represent a monistic view, one which is complementary, interconnected and interdependent. For example:

'Darkness is the absence of light,'

and

'Silence is the absence of sound.'

Yin and yang therefore represent a dynamic relationship of an indivisible whole, in which the whole is greater than the sum of the assembled parts. For example:

'A shadow cannot exist without light,'

and

'An echo cannot exist without sound.'

Bruce Lee stated:

> 'So neither gentleness nor firmness holds any more than half of a broken whole, which, fitted together, forms the true Way of Gung Fu. Gentleness/firmness is one inseparable force of one unceasing interplay of movement. They are conceived of as essentiality one, or as two coexistent forces of one indivisible whole.'

Now that you understand the true essence of yin and yang, you can start to perceive yin and yang as equal and opposite energies of an indivisible whole. For example, let's say you get into a heated argument. If the situation is managed poorly, then you may respond to aggression, i.e. yin, with agitation, frustration and even anger, which is also yin, and the whole situation will become imbalanced and escalate due to compounding energies. To re-balance the yin and yang, you could stay silent and be calming to introduce yang energy, to lower the yin energy and restore balance and harmony to the situation.

This is what Lao Tsu depicts in *Tao Te King:*

> 'Tao engenders one,
> One engenders two,
> Two engenders three,
> Three engenders all things.

> All things carry the yin while embrace the yang.
> Neutralising energy brings them into harmony.'

In this case, the Tao is one. The heated argument and silence are the two opposing yin and yang energies in the equation – two. And the way they interact to create a new outcome is three. The outcome is therefore the result of the two energies neutralising, restoring balance within the yin and yang formula, therefore maintaining harmony and happiness.

In life, our ultimate goal is to apply this philosophy of yin and yang energy management to create balance and maintain a constant state of harmony and happiness.

THE YIN AND YANG SYMBOL

Figure 4: Yin and yang symbol, known as the Taijitu

The yin and yang symbol shown above is also known as the Taijitu, which literally means **Ultimate Potential.**

The circular symbol is comprised of two colours, where black represents Yin and white represents yang.

The roundedness of the two 'fishlike' halves, seemingly flowing in motion, shows a continual interplay of the two complementary, interconnected, interdependent halves of an indivisible whole.

In each half, there is a dot of the opposite energy, symbolising that yin is rooted in yang, and yang is rooted in yin, inseparable, opposing, yet complementary and interchangeable to create a new relational state.

The challenge for us in life is to balance the Yin and Yang in everything we do, to find harmony and happiness.
As Lao Tsu describes:

> 'The Sage who is Forthright but not hurting;
> Sharp but not wounding,
> Candid but not being crude;
> Shining but not dazzling.'

However, like a full moon wanes and a new moon waxes whilst the moon remains the same, the yin and yang symbol depicts an interplay of energies, while the Tao remains ONE (as shown in the diagram below).

Figure 5: Yin and yang interplay of energy (Illustration by Lak Loi)

THE LAW OF HARMONY / THE BAMBOO PRINCIPLE

The application of the principles of yin and yang in Gung Fu are expressed as the 'Law of Harmony', also known as 'The Bamboo Principle'.

The Law of Harmony states that one should be in harmony with, not in rebellion against, the force of the opposition. This means that one should do nothing that is not natural or spontaneous; the important thing is not to strain in any way.

As Bruce Lee said:

> 'So neither gentleness nor firmness holds any more than one half of a broken whole which, welded together, forms the true way of martial art. The tendency to guard against is from getting too firm and stiff. Notice that the stiffest tree is most easily cracked, while the bamboo or willow survives by bending with the wind. This is why a Gung Fu man is soft yet not yielding, firm, yet not hard. The best example of Gung Fu is water. Water can penetrate the hardest granite because it is yielding. One cannot stab or strike at water and hurt it because that which offers no resistance cannot be overcome.'

From a combative standpoint, Bruce Lee went on to say:

> 'When the opponent expands, I contract.
> When he contracts, I expand.'

TAKE ACTION AND MASTER YOUR LIFE
THE TAO OF LIFE

The Tao of Life, or the Way of Life, is to maintain harmony by balancing the yin and yang energies in all aspects of your life. Buddhists call this the 'Middle Way' – not sad, not happy, just balanced with an appreciation for both happiness and sadness.

To do that, the Tao of Life methodology allows you to take an eagle eye perspective of your life by evaluating the balance of your life currently to identify areas that need attention so you can rebalance your life and create the future you want. The Tao of Life diagram below provides a visual snapshot and tool for your current and ideal future life. The next section explains step-by-step how to use the Tao of Life to achieve your end desires.

Question: Take five minutes to list up to eight key areas of your life. As a guideline, I have provided eight generic areas of life below:

    1. Physical.

    2. Mental.

    3. Spiritual.

    4. Financial.

    5. Social/hobbies.

    6. Career/vocation.

    7. Family and friends.

    8. Romance.

HOW TO USE THE TAO OF LIFE

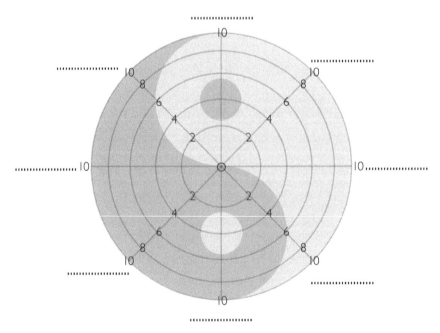

Figure 6: The Tao of Life

1. Print the Tao of Life
Download and print the Tao of Life diagram (as show in Figure 6 opposite) from www.MartialMindPower.com/Resources

2. Genius Storm Areas of Your Life
Genius storm up to eight different dimensions which are important in your life. You can use one of the following methods:

- **Key areas of your life:** physical, mental, spiritual, financial, social/hobbies, career/vocation, family and friends, romance, etc.

- **Roles you play in your life:** brother/sister, husband/wife, father/mother, friend, colleague, team player, etc.

- **Important things in your life:** financial freedom, freedom of speech, artistic expression, contribution, growth, love, environment, etc.

3. Label the Tao of Life
On each spoke of the Tao of Life, write down each area you identified in the step above.

4. Analyse Each Dimension
If you find the right balance of attention in each dimension you identified in your life, then you will also find fulfilment and gratification in them. In this step, analyse the amount of attention you're paying to each dimension, and mark a dot on the corresponding spoke on a scale from one (lowest) to ten (highest).

5. Join the Dots
Like a dot-to-dot, join the dots to see the bigger picture. Where the wheel kinks, you will be able to clearly see areas of your life you need to give more attention to re-balance your life.

6. Visualise Your Ideal Life

Now start to visualise your ideal life in all the dimensions you identified and start thinking if the score you gave should stay the same, decrease or increase. As before, draw the dots for your ideal life on the Tao of Life using a different colour so you can differentiate between the current and ideal future states.

7. Act Now!

Identify the gaps between your current and ideal future life states, and figure out what you need to do to bridge the gap by either:

- **Increasing attention** in a dimension of your life because there's currently not enough attention to it.

- **Decreasing attention** in a dimension of your life because there is currently too much time spent on it, which is sapping energy and enthusiasm from other areas of your life.

Once you have a clear idea of the gaps and how to bridge them, write down a list of simple actions that you need to take to **Achieve Your ULTIMATE POTENTIAL** and ideal future state to restore the balance in your Tao of Life, using the following as a guideline:

- **Increase attention:** What extra things do you need to start doing now?

- **Decrease attention:** What things do you need to re-prioritise, delegate to someone else or stop doing all together?

Finally, **DO IT NOW!** As Bruce Lee said:

> 'Knowing is not enough, one must apply.
> Willing is not enough, one must DO!'

To learn more about Self Mastery, pick up your copy of Master Your Life on Amazon and go to **Chapter 8: Power Side Forwards.**

SURRENDER,
NO RETREAT

THE SACRED STUDENT-TEACHER RELATIONSHIP

SIFU

In the Chinese language, the word *Sifu* refers to someone who has attained excellence in their chosen discipline through hard work over a prolonged period of time, i.e. has **cultivated excellence,** which is the true meaning of **Kung Fu.**

However, there is a common misconception that Kung Fu refers to various styles of martial arts only. In China, when you excel at something to the highest standard, you are referred to as having attained Kung Fu in that discipline, whether you are a martial artist, musician, actor, doctor, lawyer, etc.

Therefore, a Sifu is a teacher in that discipline of Kung Fu, a true role model, that takes his skill, knowledge and wisdom, and shares it with his students to educate, inspire, empower and liberate them to be the best they can, without imposing bias. As Bruce Lee stated:

> 'A good teacher protects his pupils from his own influence.'

A Sifu, therefore, has a massive responsibility to act selflessly in the best interests of his students at all times.

WHEN THE STUDENT IS READY, THE TEACHER APPEARS

There is a famous proverb:

> 'When the student is ready,
> The teacher appears.'

There is a firm belief that when you set your intention and act through the concentration of your will, then that which you wish for comes true.

When I wanted to learn Bruce Lee's martial art and philosophy, believe it or not I did not know Bruce had actually left his teachings behind following his untimely passing, nor did I know he had called his martial philosophy and process 'Jeet Kune Do'. All I knew was that my intuition was compelling me to find and learn Bruce's teachings – I was not even sure why at that time.

In the early noughties, Google was in its infancy, and other well-established search engines like Lycos and Netscape had little to no information on 'Bruce Lee', let alone 'Jeet Kune Do'. I searched for months with no success.

At the time, I was working as an IT Consultant in Manhattan, and as an avid gym-goer, I would frequent the nearest health club. One day I was consulting in mid-town and after work I popped into the local gym. I remember walking past the studio on my left, and from the corner of my eye, the words 'Learn Bruce Lee's Martial Art' vividly popped out at me, written on a scruffy white A4 piece of paper stuck on the studio window. I turned abruptly, snapping my head round to read it… and lo and behold, Jeet Kune Do classes were held there every Monday and Thursday evening. I can confidently say, I willed it so hard that my teacher finally appeared.

And just like that, when the student is truly ready, your teacher will appear in the form that will best serve you based on your intentions and will. Remember to stay alert and aware; you never know how that sign may appear (literally in my case).

WHEN THE STUDENT IS UNREADY, THE TEACHER DISAPPEARS

There can also come a time in your student-teacher journey when the student turns from 'ready' to 'unready'.

In my experience, several things can be the root cause of the student becoming 'unready', which include:

- The student 'knows it all', and there is nothing else the teacher can teach. As Bruce Lee said:

  'The usefulness of the teacup is in its emptiness.'

- The student dishonours another student, the teacher, the school, its property and/or the code of honour, and no longer is deemed fit to be a student and represent the teacher and/or the school.

- The teachings are no longer having a positive impact on the student, and the teacher can no longer help the student.

That is when the teacher retreats by withdrawing his services and liberates the student from the student-teacher bond.

WHEN THE TEACHER IS READY, THE STUDENT APPEARS

There are three learning positions in order of advancement, which are:

1. Student.

2. Teacher.

3. Observer or examiner.

For every student who aspires to become a teacher one day, having trained for years, invested extensive time, effort and energy to cultivate his skills and knowledge, developing the foundations for excellence, the time to move onto the second learning position as a teacher is an honour and a privilege when it eventually arrives.

And when the new teacher finally qualifies to teach, they pluck up the courage to put themselves out there and pass on their skills and experience, and decide to set up their school and put the word out that they are **open to teach.**

A new intention is set with the power of the teacher's will to spread his light to illuminate paths for new students, so they too can cultivate Kung Fu in the discipline they have chosen to specialise in. The time for the teacher to educate, inspire, empower and liberate others selflessly is upon them.

As I like to say:

> 'If you build it, they will come,'

…and new students most certainly will start to appear, just like I showed up.

WHEN THE TEACHER IS UNREADY, THE STUDENT DISAPPEARS

And finally, there can also come a time when the teacher has served his purpose, and no longer adds any value to the student, so it is time for the student to retreat.

In my experience, several things can be the root cause of the teacher becoming 'unready', which include:

- The student has completed the course.

- The student is no longer progressing, for example, their peer group has left and they have no one suitable to train with.

- The teacher does not have Kung Fu and is not fit, qualified and/or experienced enough to teach.

- The teacher is abusing their power and authority over the student.

- The teacher is acting in a selfish and/or rude manner.

- The teacher is casting his/her own influence on the student, potentially corrupting the values and virtues of the teachings.

That is when the student retreats by withdrawing their surrender to the teacher and liberates the teacher from the student-teacher bond.

SURRENDER, NO RETREAT

I am a firm believer that a teacher should not aim to keep students for life, but to **equip them with the ability to think, so they are liberated.**

The foundations of a student-teacher relationship are built on **surrender,** which has implicit **mutual respect** and **trust.**

The student must appear with an open mind. As Bruce Lee famously said:

> 'The usefulness of the teacup is in its emptiness.'

Without the student's surrender with an open mind and unconditional trust in the intention and ability of the teacher to help cultivate his Kung Fu, there is no hope of pouring the teacher's tea into the student's teacup for him to taste. Of course, the student must do his due diligence to find the right school and teacher for them before they surrender to join the school.

Bruce Lee believed:

> 'A teacher is never a giver of the truth;
> He is a guide, a pointer to the truth,
> That each student must find himself.'

Likewise, without the teacher's surrender with a selfless and unbiased excellence to help the student cultivate their Kung Fu, the student will be reluctant to taste the teacher's new tea. Likewise, the teacher must also do his due diligence to evaluate whether the student will be a right fit for him and the school before they surrender and take the student on.

It all starts with an unconditional surrender from both the teacher and the student. And when there is no surrender, then one of them will eventually retreat (or disappear).

Steve Jobs hit the nail on the head when he famously said:

> 'Treat your employees [or students] so well
> That they don't want to leave.'

I say:

> 'Surrender, No Retreat.'

TAKE ACTION AND MASTER YOUR LIFE
THE ART OF SURRENDER

Learn the Art of Surrender by following these ten top tips…

For Students

1. Empty your teacup so you can taste new tea. Open your mind with humbleness and humility, and do not show off.

2. Respect and trust your fellow students/training partners and teacher (until they give you a 'just' reason not to) and immerse yourself in the community to get the best out of your experiential learning. Remember, when your training partners/teacher can no longer serve you, you have the right to retreat.

3. Be grateful for the teachings you are receiving. Even the negative experiences are your teachers. For example, when you get hit or you get your ass kicked during sparring, you end up with bruises and bumps – these are all part of the process.

4. Detach yourself from outcomes, and be gentle on yourself, allowing yourself sufficient time and space to learn and grow.

5. Walk before you can run. Perfect practice calmly makes perfect; imperfect practice rushed takes more time to correct. And remember, keep practising.

6. Respect the school, its code of honour and property at all times.

7. The more you put in, the more you will get out, so work hard, fight easy.

8. Remember martial arts are a way of life, so take your lessons from the dojo and apply them to all areas of your life, which include: justice, courage, benevolence, politeness, honesty and sincerity, honour, loyalty, character and self-control.

9. Look for the lesson in every experience and keep growing throughout your whole life.

10. Go with the flow.

For Teachers

1. Treat each student as if they are a loving member of your family, with a duty of care and responsibility for their health, safety and wellbeing.

2. Act through love, not fear, even when you are disciplining your students.

3. Act selflessly to genuinely help your students learn, grow and prosper, getting your own biases and influences out of the way.

4. Respect your students and teachers at all times, even if you have conflicts with their personalities. Remember, when you can no longer serve your student/teacher, you have the right to retreat your service to them.

5. Respect your own school's code of honour – no one likes a hypocrite.

6. Remember one day you will get old, so nurture students who will want to hold your hand in your old age.

7. Let your ego go and aim to make your students better than you.

8. Give the students wings so one day they can fly on their own.

9. Look for the lesson in every experience and keep growing throughout your whole life.

10. Go with the flow.

KOBAYASHI MARU

WHAT'S IT GOING TO BE, WIN OR LOSE?

LOSE-LOSE

The *Kobayashi Maru* is a training exercise in the fictional *Star Trek* universe designed to test the character of Starfleet Academy cadets in a no-win scenario.

The Kobayashi Maru test was first depicted in the opening scene of the film *Star Trek II: The Wrath of Khan* and also appears in the 2009 film Star Trek. Screenwriter Jack B. Sowards is credited with inventing the test. The test's name is occasionally used among Star Trek fans to describe a no-win scenario, a test of one's character or a solution that involves redefining the problem.

The notional primary goal of the exercise is to rescue the civilian vessel Kobayashi Maru in a simulated battle with the Klingons. The disabled ship is located in the Klingon Neutral Zone, and any Starfleet ship entering the zone would cause an interstellar incident.

The approaching cadet crew must decide whether to attempt rescue of the Kobayashi Maru crew, endangering their own ship and lives, or leave the Kobayashi Maru to certain destruction. If the cadets choose to attempt rescue, the simulation is designed to guarantee that the cadets' ship is destroyed with the loss of all crew members.

[Excerpt from Wikipedia. Edited by Lak Loi.]

EFFORT IS FUTILE, NO EFFORT IS FUTILE

Have you ever been in a situation where you are trying really hard to achieve a certain goal, and frustratingly, you do not seem to be getting any closer? Effort seems futile.

You may experience a surging sensation to give up altogether and not even bother anymore, which certainly ensures you won't get there. No effort also seems futile.

It seems like a stalemate. Now what?

TO YOU, THROUGH YOU

I am a firm believer that everything you are meant to do or not meant to do comes **to you, through you** at the right time. Any strain or tension just puts that thing you're trying to achieve plainly out of reach.

You may have heard the saying:

'Everything happens for a reason.'

I prefer to say:

'Everything that happens, happens for a reason.
Everything that does not happen, does not happen for a reason.'

So why fight it?

LEARN THE ART OF DYING

Bruce Lee spoke about 'Learning the Art of Dying'. He was not speaking literally, but metaphorically, of letting go of the past and releasing any limiting beliefs so you can once again become a fluid human in the present moment. Bruce said:

'Like everyone else, you want to learn the way to win,
But never to accept the way to lose, to accept defeat.
To learn to die is to be liberated from it.
So when tomorrow comes,
You must free your ambitious mind, and
Learn the art of dying.'

Bruce was constantly practising this idea of dying, because to him it meant returning to the 'beginner's mind' and the 'centre of the nucleus' – the starting point from which everything grows outwardly. He even had a tombstone commissioned as a piece of artwork, with an epitaph which read,

> 'In memory of a once fluid man,
> Crammed and distorted by the classical mess.'

He used this as a physical reminder to let go of any rigidity that prevents growth or movement, which causes literal death of body, mind and spirit. After all, when movement in our body goes, humans suffer from 'rigor mortis' which literally means 'stiffness of death'.

Bruce went on to say:

> 'To understand and live now,
> There must be a dying to everything of yesterday.
> Die continually to every newly gained experience.
> Be in a state of choiceless awareness of what is.'

Dying, in this instance, is more about living in the moment and being able to continue being the eternal student to learn and grow. Bruce also said:

> 'Drop and dissolve inner blockage,
> A conditioned mind is never a free mind.
> Wipe away and dissolve all its experience and
> Be born afresh.
>
> Like everyone else, you want to learn the way to win,
> But never to learn the way to lose.
> To accept defeat, to learn to die,
> Is to be liberated from it.

Once you accept this you are free to flow and to harmonise.
Fluidity is the way to an empty mind.
You must free your ambitious mind and
Learn the art of dying.'

And then all there is left to do is to do your best. Remember:

At the peak of your effort there is a dying.
Only then does 'it' happen or not happen,
If 'it' is meant to happen or not happen.

BATTLES AND WARS

Sun Tzu stated:

'If you know the enemy and know yourself,
You need not fear the result of a hundred battles.

If you know yourself but not the enemy,
For every victory gained you will also suffer a defeat.

If you know neither the enemy nor yourself,
You will succumb in every battle.'

Life is full of battles and wars. Your first enemy is yourself —
knowing your own body, mind and spirit. Only once you have
mastered your own faculties will you be prepared to take on
enemies outside yourself. These are not necessarily people,
but challenges life presents for you to self-realise, because that's
what life is all about. And just like the Kobayashi Maru test,
'it builds and tests your character.'

Life can seem like one big war unless you conquer yourself through
cultivating Self Mastery. You will realise how to pick your battles
carefully, because not all battles are meant to be fought, let alone
won. You may have heard the saying:

'You may have lost the battle,
But won the war.'

As your consciousness rises through cultivating your Self Mastery, you will realise that there never was a battle or war to be fought in the first place. Everything is just as it is meant to be. The Kobayashi Maru is merely an illusion of a problem with no solution, a lose-lose situation with no way out. So all that is left to do is to always **do your best and work peacefully.**

TAKE ACTION AND MASTER YOUR LIFE
LEARN THE ART OF DYING

1. Practise being in the present moment.

2. Let go of the past and release any limiting beliefs.

3. Identify areas of your life where you are being rigid.

4. Identify how you can be more flexible and accommodating to what's happening or not happening in your life.

5. Identify any firm attachment and desire to something or someone.

6. Create some space between you and your attachments to start freeing yourself to become more fluid.

7. Ask yourself, are you doing your best? If not, then simply, do better.

TRAIN NOTHING, ACHIEVE EVERYTHING

LESS IS MORE

ISOMETRIC EXERCISES

Isometric exercises are based on resistance training in a static position, for example holding a plank or sitting in a 90-degree squat position. Over a prolonged period of time (oftentimes 60 seconds or more), you start to feel pressure, heaviness, fatigue, and your muscles start to shake.

TOO HARD, TOO STRONG

When students start practising martial arts, they're usually too hard and too heavy. Sometimes because they're unknowingly driven by the ego, trying to prove to themselves and to others that they're strong and powerful, and mostly because they lack proper command and control of their physical faculties. This oftentimes leads to slow and clunky movement despite the desperate attempt at making it 'look good'.

Have you ever tried to open a door which looked heavy, and you almost take it off its hinges, nearly smashing it to smithereens because it was much lighter than the eyes and brain computed it to be? You used far more strength than was necessary to open the door.

THE WORD

I asked some students to use one word to describe the feeling of training too hard, too strong, and they all agreed on the word:

Resistance.

FEELING LIFE

I asked some students: if you carried yourself through daily life over-exerting yourself by being too hard and too strong all the time, as in your beginner martial arts training, allowing resistance to creep into your mind and body, how would that make you feel? And they said:

- Stressed.

- Tense.

- Sad.

- Depressed.

- Angry.

- Frustrated.

LIGHTENING FLUIDITY

As students' techniques improve, they develop speed and fluidity. To develop speed, you need to relax and only recruit the muscle fibres that are absolutely necessary to facilitate that particular movement (agonist muscles) and switch off those muscle fibres (antagonist muscles) that'd otherwise slow that movement down throughout the muscle action sequencing/steps. Since speed is proportionate to power, power also increases. I call it:

'Lightening Fluidity'

meaning a light, effortless ease of movement, with lightning speed and power and smooth, graceful motion – all at the same time.

AWARENESS ROOTS

Before you can address the problems resistance can create in life, you have to become aware that resistance exists in the first place.

Resistance in the mind and body always appears as illness and dis-ease, sometimes silent (such as coronary heart disease), stress being one of the major causes for most Western illnesses including cancer (inflammation of cells under resistance causing imbalance in homeostasis).

Once you have clarity on how resistance is manifesting itself in your mind and body, only then can you withdraw to your inner self to ask yourself: what is the root cause of all this resistance?

And only once you gain clarity on that can you start to think about how you are going to resolve your resistance problem(s).

Remember:

'What you resist,
Persists.'

So:

'To get a different outcome,
We have to do something different.'

THE BOAT ON THE TOXIC LAKE

Relaxation is all about releasing resistance once you know the root cause of it. Usually, it is not about what you need to do, rather, it's usually about what you should **not do.**

Imagine you're rowing a boat across a toxic lake. Would you scoop up the toxic sludge from the lake into your boat? Of course you would not, as it would make you ill or kill you, whether from being exposed to the toxicity or from drowning in it when your boat sinks.

Your mind is like the boat, and you have a choice of making an effort to scoop that toxic sludge into your boat or **do nothing** and allow it to stay where it is – outside your boat. The paradox here is that to become immune to resistance, we have to learn to train to do nothing (in such situations), just as in training our martial arts techniques to develop 'Lightening Fluidity'.

LESS IS MORE

And just like that, you realise that a lot of the time, we are training to do less so we can achieve more. Be it in the body when training martial arts, or in the mind when living life, we need to learn to:

Train Nothing,
Achieve Everything.

TAKE ACTION AND MASTER YOUR LIFE
TRAIN NOTHING, ACHIEVE EVERYTHING

1. Seek your resistance.

2. Accept your resistance.

3. Seek the root cause of your resistance.

4. Identify:

   • What you need to do, and more importantly,

   • What you need to stop doing to reduce and/or eliminate your resistance.

5. Keep practising 'doing nothing' until your resistance completely goes away and you are 'whole, healed and happy'.

6. Rinse and repeat from step #1 for all your resistances.

ALL FOR NOTHING

IN THE NOTHINGNESS, LIES EVERYTHING

CONTAGION

This chapter was written at the beginning of the coronavirus pandemic in March 2020, which has swept the world.

People are falling ill left, right and centre, hospitals are at max. capacity with casualties suffering the ill effects of the virus (sore throats, coughing, fevers, shortness of breath, time in intensive care), permanent after-effects (loss of smell and taste, to name just a couple), and worse still... death is rife.

Countries have come to a total standstill, economies and markets are tanking, the social norms have totally collapsed with global communities being put into isolation, and some governments are unleashing martial law (in some countries) to police and further prevent the spread of the disease.

Though the media is doing its best to educate the global populous about the virus and its ill effects, and to prevent it spreading by instructing people to stay at home and adopt greater hygiene practices, people have been put into a state of frightened frenzy.

SURVIVAL MODE

As primal beings, when we experience fear, especially from something like a pandemic that threatens your health, livelihood, life, loved ones and the potential existence of humankind, our primal survival mode kicks in hardcore.

The virus has catapulted us head-first into survival mode through the following triggers:

- People scared of catching the virus and getting ill or dying.

- Worry for loved ones' health and lives,
  especially for the frail, elderly and vulnerable.

- Anxiety about the loss of income and livelihoods.

- Scared of lockdown and presence of martial law.

- Scared of being in one's own company in isolation.

- The sense of feeling imprisoned in one's own
  home and getting bored and/or cabin fever.

- Uncertainty of what is happening,
  and fear of the unknown future.

- Eerie abandoned streets, reminiscent of a zombie
  apocalypse movie.

- Fear of not having enough resources to survive.

- The surreality of reality as the illusory house of cards
  seems to be falling down and the fabric of life is changing.

When we go into survival mode, most people have a natural tendency to protect themselves first and foremost. Everyone and everything else tend to come second.

Our first action is to protect ourselves from the impending threat, so people have gone out and bought their protective armour by way of face masks, plastic gloves and anti-bacterial hand gels and sanitisers.

Second, we hoard as many resources as possible such as food, drink and even toilet paper, so we can hide in safety and have enough to survive without going back out into the looming danger.

THE IRONY

The irony with something like a pandemic is:

- When a few people hoard all the protective gear, the rest won't have any and will simply have no choice but to go without and risk spreading and perpetuating the disease, increasing the risk to those with protective gear, so no one benefits.

- If everyone didn't decide to panic-buy and start stockpiling resources, there would be enough to go round as usual, rather than triggering more fear and panic.

Our survival mode has created a 'mass hysteria'. For example, I watched a man being interviewed on a TV news report outside a supermarket carrying several multipacks of toilet roll. The journalist asked:

> "Why have you bought so many toilet rolls?"

The man replied:

> "I don't know.
> Everyone else was buying them,
> So I thought I'd get some as well."

In a nutshell, when people go into survival mode, most people will act with what I call 'Emotional Dumbness', because they are no longer thinking consciously. Rather, their cognitive processes bypass their conscious faculties and operate from their primal survival mode centre in the mid-brain, called the amygdala.

EVERYTHING

The human race can act through one of two modalities:

   1. **Fear,** or

   2. **Love.**

When we act through fear, we look at the world through a negative lens of paranoia and scarcity. This is when we sink into **Survival Mode** and act selfishly through our lowest vibration.

When we act through love, we look at the world through a positive lens of kindness, compassion and abundance. This is when we rise to the occasion in **Service Mode** and act selflessly and demonstrate true inspired thought-leadership in our highest vibration.

To flip our mindsets from Survival Mode to Service Mode, we can practise 'The Art of Gratitude'.

When you show gratitude for what you have, rather than fixating on what you do not have, an unusual mental shift takes place inside you. There is a sudden realisation that you are already blessed, are enough, have enough. Desire for taking dissolves, and you switch to a mode of giving.

Why not try 'The Art of Gratitude' exercise in the 'Take Action and Master Your Life' section, and see what happens for yourself?

NOTHINGNESS

It is weird and wonderful that:

In order to **keep everything**
(that we already have and can be grateful for)

We literally have to **do nothing.**

This calls for the action of inaction. If we do nothing and go nowhere, the virus cannot transfer and spread and will eventually die out, and the human race will survive.

We have to embrace staying in, not as self-isolation, but self-liberation. It is a once-in-a-lifetime opportunity when everything outside is quiet for us to be silent inside, so we can:

Disconnect to reconnect.

We can achieve this through meditation, to connect to our higher selves towards our self-realisation, and as a side-benefit, we'll increase our relaxation and boost our immune systems to fend off the virus and recover speedily in the event that we contract it.

And whilst in self-isolation, we can use this opportunity not only to connect to our higher selves – we are also gifted an opportunity to reconnect with our household members as we get to spend more time with them. We can take the extra time to catch up with family and friends we have lost touch with while we were consumed in the 'business of busyness' of daily life.

Meditating also teaches us that we are not our thoughts. Has someone ever enraged you so much that you thought you wanted to kill them, but (hopefully) you didn't? This is because you are not defined by your thoughts; rather your character is cultivated by your outward expression of your thoughts, otherwise most people would have done some jail time or be dead for living out every negative thought they ever experienced.

When you connect to your higher self, you learn to sit in a place of Zen. So, when a tornado like this pandemic comes, you can sit in the eye of the storm where everything is still whilst the chaos swirls around you, and maintain your centre, calm, clarity and calibration of thoughts and actions/inactions.

When you act through love and the service mode, you realise that we are all in this together and no one is immune to this horrid virus. And there is a stark realisation that the only way to beat this is together as one global family. In the words of the Three Musketeers:

'All for one,
One for all.'

I saw a humorous meme, which summed this up nicely:

'For the first time in history,
We can save the human race and the world
By laying in front of a TV and doing nothing.
Let's not screw this up.'

IN THE NOTHINGNESS, LIES EVERYTHING

A pandemic like this can bring the worst and best out of people, depending on which lens we are wearing.

This is a time to put on the love lens, for when we do that, we learn that:

- **We are one,** as we can only beat this virus if we act as one global family to stop its spread.

- **We are equal,** as this virus does not discriminate by colour, creed, race, religion, gender, sexual orientation, religion or political preference.

- **We have strength of character,** when we act with patience over panic, to make wise decisions and actions/inactions.

- **We have free will,** and can act with selflessness over selfishness.

- **We can heal Mother Earth,** by simply self-isolating and allowing Mother Earth's atmosphere, waterways and lands to recover and rejuvenate.

- **We are not in control,** as an invisible enemy threatens our health, livelihoods and lives, and puts our egos into check.

- **We are spiritual beings,** when you start fearing death and the illusion of your reality starts to fall apart – this puts the love of God back into us when all else fails.

- **Life is more precious than material things,** when we realise what really matters most is the health and wellbeing of ourselves and our loved ones.

- **We are custodians** of one another, other sentient beings and Mother Earth.

MARTIAL MIND POWER

As martial artists, we train to conquer our fear so we don't have to act through our primal survival mode. Rather, we can act with emotional intelligence because we have cultivated mastery over our physiological fear mechanism to develop deep calmness and crystal-clear clarity when put in the face of adversity and act with strength of character, leadership and wisdom, cool composure and calibration.

We train to understand how to sit in the eye of the storm, where it is Zen, while the chaos swirls around us like a tornado. This allows us to make wise, informed choices, allowing us to rise up to help people sucked into the tornado spinning out of control.

As martial artists, we train through gruelling pain and suffering, enduring many bruises and injuries (i.e. dis-ease – the absence of ease), only to come to learn that:

'After every dis-ease,
Comes ease.'

This is the time for martial artists to rise to the occasion in service mode and help humankind get through the fear of this virus by using our Martial Mind Power.

I like to think of this pandemic virus as a divine gift, which is:

'Not a great disaster,
But a great corrector.'

And remember, when you wear the love lens, you will see this:

'Not as the end,
But as a new beginning,'

Because it is:

'All for nothing.'

A poem by Laura Kelly Fannuci sums this up beautifully:

'When this is over,
May we never again
Take for granted:
A handshake with a stranger;
Full shelves at the store;
Conversations with neighbours;
A crowded theatre;
Friday night out;
The taste of communion;
A routine check-up;
The school rush each morning;
Coffee with a friend;
The stadium roaring;
Each deep breath;
A boring Tuesday;
Life itself.

When this ends,
May we find,
That we have become
More like the people
We wanted to be,
We were called to be,
We hoped to be,
And may we stay
That way – better
For each other
Because of the worst.'

TAKE ACTION AND MASTER YOUR LIFE
THE ART OF GRATITUDE

To develop a sense of gratitude for all that we have been blessed with, and act from a place of love and servitude, we have to simply sit in peace and quiet, and be grateful for our:

1. Physical Body
Give thanks and gratitude for your health and wellbeing. Even if you have contracted the virus and are feeling sick, you can be grateful for still being alive. Have faith in yourself, that you can beat the virus and live a healthy and happy life hereafter.

2. Mental Body
Give thanks and gratitude for your ability to think and become. For what we conceive and believe, we can achieve. We have the power within us to heal ourselves by thinking it so, so keep your mind strong and steadfast.

3. Spiritual Body

Give thanks and gratitude for your unbreakable human spirit. Through our inner 'conscious will', we can change our outer reality through pure intention, focused energy and our indomitable fighting spirit.

4. Social Life

Give thanks and gratitude for your community, hobbies and interests that bring meaning and purpose to your life.

5. Family, Friends and Colleagues

Give thanks and gratitude for your family, friends and colleagues that bring love, connection and magic into your life.

6. Romance

Give thanks and gratitude for your partner and all their unconditional love and support, through sickness and health, through rich and poor.

7. Career and Vocation

Give thanks and gratitude for your career. If you are able to work from home, then give thanks to your IT departments for facilitating remote working. If you lost your job recently, then give thanks and gratitude for everything they did do, and the time to pursue that thing which you always wanted to do but never had the time till now – could be as simple as taking some much deserved rest and relaxation.

8. Finance

Give thanks and gratitude for having a roof over your head, food on your table and clean clothes on your back, and if you have cash in the bank, give thanks and gratitude for that too.

ZEN IN THE ART OF FIGHTING

EYE OF THE STORM

WHEN ANGER ARRIVES, SKILL LEAVES

When someone or something triggers fear or anger in you, and your heartbeat rises above 135 beats per minute, you lose all control of conscious rational thinking and go into an unconscious 'survival mode'.

This is all part of our animalistic, primal adrenal reaction, designed to help humans over 20,000 years ago fight against or flee from sabretooth tigers and other predators that threatened human life.

When fear or anger rises, you will physiologically experience:

- **Pre-fight or flight shakes:** The adrenal dump is like nitrous in a street race car, jacking up your performance for fight or flight, causing your body to shake.

- **Voice quiver:** When you fight or flee, there is no need to talk but simply put all your energy into your mechanical performance to incapacitate the threat or danger. If you forcefully try and say something, your voice will quiver under the adrenalised conditions.

- **Dry mouth:** You no longer need to eat and break down food with the saliva in your mouth, so your salivary glands will switch off.

- **Tunnel vision:** Your eyes will constrict like a hunter honing in on its prey, so you will not be able to see people in your mid-to-wide peripheral vision.

- **Temporary deafness:** You will not hear people shouting around you in the noise of all the fear- and anger-induced adrenaline running riot inside your body and mind.

- **Sweaty palms and forehead:** To help you cool down as your heart begins to pump faster, increasing your core temperature.

- **Nausea:** The feeling of butterflies in the pit of your belly from the adrenal dump into your bloodstream.

- **Bowel and bladder loosening:** To allow you to excrete unnecessary bodily liquids and solids, to make you lighter so you can run or fight faster.

- **Loss of appetite:** This is no time to eat, so all your blood flow is diverted away from your digestive system and redirected towards your muscles for optimal physical performance.

- **Increased heart rate:** To prime your muscles for optimal mechanical performance, more blood flow is sent to them.

- **Time distortion:** Time can appear to stand still. Ever heard the statement, 'It all seemed to happen so fast' or 'Everything seemed to be in slow motion'? Your brain speeds up in an adrenalised state, and it seems as if things are moving slower, but in fact you are processing at a vastly greater rate than usual.

- **Restless sleep:** The slow release of adrenaline after an adrenalised confrontation will keep you up at night, because all that energy in your bloodstream is not being used up and can cause agitation and jitters.

- **Sadness and depression:** From the shame and guilt that comes from getting into an unresourceful state, putting your worst side forwards, and from the grave outcomes a fight may have, be it insult, injury or even death.

Behaviourally, you will experience:

- **Erratic eye movement:** Looking out for attackers, the police, CCTV cameras, public witnesses and possible rescuers.

- **Adrenal reaction:** Pale face, eyes wide open from adrenaline-induced tunnel vision, stern facial expression, fidgeting in an attempt to hide the adrenal shake (like a cold 'shiver'), voice may quiver nervously.

- **Posturing and splaying arms:** Used to make you appear bigger before an attack to intimidate the other person, like a bear under attack.

- **Beckoning finger:** Beckoning victims on with your finger.

- **Nodding head and neck pecking:** Nodding your head and pecking your neck like a cockerel to protect your throat, which is a primary target.

- **Eye bulge:** Eyes may appear wide and staring due to adrenaline-induced tunnel vision.

- **Drooped eyebrows:** Eyebrows lowered to protect eyes.

- **'Stancing up':** You may take up an innate fighting stance and hide your major organs from attack.

- **Closedown distance:** As aggression builds, you will close down the distance with more erratic movement.

- **Concealed hands:** It's not always the case, but you may conceal your hands if you're hiding a weapon.

- **Limited vocabulary:** Your vocabulary reduces to singular words the closer you get to striking someone or something out of sheer anger and rage.

If you happen to engage in physical combat, once you have lost your senses (literally, as described above), the only techniques you will have are those that are embedded within the deepest caverns of your subconscious. If you have not trained your martial arts body and mind faculties enough to embed the teachings into your neuro-physiological depths, what will come out will be what I call 'bear-cat fighting' – that is, your untrained, animalistic, primal reactions, which will be skill-less. You will literally behave like a threatened animal.

Daniel Goleman, the author of the famous book *Emotional Intelligence: Why It Can Matter More Than IQ,* describes how anger alters your behaviour in this beautiful short story:

> 'A belligerent samurai, an old Japanese tale goes, once challenged a Zen master to explain the concept of heaven and hell. The monk replied with scorn, "You're nothing but a lout – I can't waste my time with the likes of you!"
>
> His very honour attacked, the samurai flew into a rage and, pulling his sword from its scabbard, yelled, "I could kill you for your impertinence."
>
> "That," the monk calmly replied, "is hell."
>
> Startled at seeing the truth in what the master pointed out about the fury that had him in its grip, the samurai calmed down, sheathed his sword, and bowed, thanking the monk for the insight.
>
> "And that," said the monk "is heaven."
>
> The sudden awakening of the samurai to his own agitated state illustrates the crucial difference between being caught up in a feeling and becoming aware that you are being swept away by it. Socrates's injunction, "Know thyself," speaks to the keystone of emotional intelligence: awareness of one's own feelings as they occur.'

There is a famous quote by Aristotle that goes:

'Anybody can become angry – that is easy;
But to be angry with the right person,
And to the right degree,
And at the right time,
And for the right purpose,
And in the right way –
That is not within everybody's power and is not easy.'

For if you do not handle yourself with emotional intelligence, the moment anger arrives, skill leaves.

THERE IS NO OPPONENT

In the limited edition version of Bruce Lee's blockbuster movie Enter the Dragon, there is an opening scene with a beautiful dialogue between Bruce Lee (as 'Lee') and a Shaolin Abbot. The dialogue, written by Bruce Lee himself, wherein he is conveying a lesson about the highest state of a martial artist, is as follows...

Lee: Teacher.

Shaolin Abbott: I see your talents have gone beyond the mere physical level. Your skills are now at the point of spiritual insight. I have several questions. What is the highest technique you hope to achieve?

Lee: To have no technique.

Shaolin Abbott: Very good. What are your thoughts when facing an opponent?

Lee: There is no opponent.

Shaolin Abbott: And why is that?

Lee: Because the word "I" does not exist.

Shaolin Abbott: So, continue...

Lee: A good fight should be like a small play, but played seriously. A good martial artist does not become tense, but ready. Not thinking, yet not dreaming. Ready for whatever may come. When the opponent expands, I contract. When he contracts, I expand. And when there is an opportunity, I do not hit, it hits all by itself.

Shaolin Abbott: Now, you must remember, the enemy has only images and illusions behind which he hides his true motives. Destroy the image and you will break the enemy. The 'it' that you refer to is a powerful weapon easily misused by the martial artist who deserts his vows. For centuries now, the code of the Shaolin Temple has been preserved. Remember, the honour of our brotherhood has been held true. Tell me now the Shaolin Commandment number thirteen?

Lee: A martial artist has to take responsibility for himself and accept the consequences of his own doing.

This dialogue embodies what I call the 1,000:10,000 rule. That is, to cultivate a technique, you must practise it perfectly a thousand times. For the technique to become an unconscious intelligent response, which is much quicker than a conscious reaction, you must practise it perfectly ten thousand times.

As Bruce Lee went on to say:

'I do not fear the man that has practised 10,000 kicks once, I fear the man that has practised one kick 10,000 times.'

EYE OF THE STORM

When there is a tornado, there is chaos and destruction everywhere except in the eye of the storm. This is the epicentre of the tornado, where it is totally tranquil.

Combat is like being in a tornado. The untrained fighter's emotions get caught up in the swirling chaos of fear and anger which destroys everything in its path. The trained fighter, on the other hand, will sit in the eye of the storm, totally Zen, able to keep their heartrate below 135 bpm avoiding the adrenal reaction, able to see all the chaos swirling around him without any emotional reaction and able to respond intelligently as he sees everything in his calm, calibrated and composed stature.

Daniel Goleman called this 'Emotional Intelligence', which is the foundation for 'The Art of Fighting Without Fighting'.

THE TARGET HIT ME

One of the key principles in the Zen martial art of archery called Kyudo is a practice of 'non-aiming'. It probably sounds ludicrous to a Westerner, who if handed a bow, arrow and target will try hard to hit the target for their own self-gratification. Let me explain…

Kyudo is the art of being one with the universe, connecting Mother Earth and Heaven through one's body, mind, spirit, bow, arrow and the target through the practice of 'The Eight Stages', described as follows:

    1. Ashibumi – establishing footing with
      a solid grounded foundation.

2. **Dozukuri** – correcting the posture, grounding your energetic-self to Mother Earth and Heaven, and finding your spiritual centre.

3. **Yugamae** – readying the bow and becoming one with it and sending your spirit to the target before shooting.

4. **Uchiokoshi** – raising the bow, turning the handle on the door to the universe.

5. **Daisan and Hikiwake** – drawing the bow, opening the door to the universe. The storm starts to rage under the tension of the bow and the string.

6. **Kai** – completing the draw and peeking your head through the door of the universe. Your head placed inside the drawn bow, you stand in complete Zen-ness in the eye of the storm, surrounded by all the storm's tension in the bow and string whilst holding the arrow in perfect balance and harmony.

7. **Hanare** – the release: when you meet the moment of Zen, the target comes to you and the arrow releases all by itself, to establish…

8. **Zanshin** – 'remaining spirit', which is when you 'send the spirit forth' through the door of the universe to 'become one with it', even after the arrow has hit the target.

If a Kyudoka is aiming, he puts attainment of Zen firmly out of his reach when he is:

• Fixated on one point of a target, exercising rigid control to hit the target all by himself. This shows an abandonment of trust and surrender to the universe's ability to guide him there.

- Using muscular power and tension rather than his bio-mechanical efficiency to naturally draw the bow with a relaxed firmness, and firm relaxedness.

- Attached to the egocentric glory of hitting the bullseye, rather than becoming one with the target and allowing it to hit the arrow all by itself.

To master Kyudo then, one has to learn to relax, trust, surrender, let go, and to be one with everything – physically, mentally and spiritually.

FIGHT FIRE WITH WATER

As they say,

'You cannot fight fire with fire.'

You need water to douse fire.

Likewise, don't fight strength with strength, else you will drain all your energy and potentially be overpowered by a foe who is stronger than you.

Bruce Lee spoke about there being five types of fighters, as follows:

1. **Runner** – Someone who is nimble on their feet, dances around a lot and comes into the fighting measure momentarily with a few quick strikes before escaping to safety outside the fighting measure again.

2. **Touch and Go** – A tactile fighter who blocks then hits.

3. **Crasher** – Someone who will steamroll right through you like a bull.

4. Shooter – Someone who wants to take you down to the ground and grapple you into a submission, break or until you pass out/die.

5. Interceptor – Someone who will wait for his opponent to strike first, then intercept their attack with their own, which also acts as a defence.

The key to successful combat is to recognise the type of fighter you are facing within the first few seconds of the fight, assessing the foe's movements to understand their modus operandi, and then to use tactics and strategies to break them down—this is the trademark of an intelligent fighter.

When you learn to fight intelligently through studying and training in each and every one of these fighting attributes:

- All ranges of combat – close, medium and long.

- All modalities – standing, taking down and on the ground.

- With and without weapons – as an extension of your limb weapons.

Only then will you truly understand all the moves in this combative game of chess. Once you have learnt the moves, you can start to truly play, but play seriously (as Bruce Lee said).

THE TALE OF THE DRAGON AND THE WOOD CUTTER

Bob Bremer was one of Bruce Lee's famous private students who trained over a thousand hours in Bruce's backyard, and was a member of Bruce's LA Chinatown Jeet Kune Do school for two years. It was during one of Bob's private Jeet Kune Do lessons that Bruce told him this fable, which is published by Tim Tackett in his recent book Essential Jeet Kune Do:

> 'Once upon a time there was an old Chinese woodcutter. He was very poor. Every day, he went out to the forest hoping to chop enough wood to sell in the town to make enough money to buy rice to feed his family. One day when he was deep in the forest cutting down a tree with his trusty axe, he heard a giant roar from behind on the other side of the clearing. He heard the roar again and saw that the trees were shaking as if there was a huge windstorm. Since the wind was calm where he was, he couldn't figure out what was happening on the other side of the clearing.
>
> He soon found out because a huge dragon suddenly appeared. The woodcutter immediately thought to himself, "If I could kill this dragon, I could sell it for so much money that I could feed my family for the rest of my life and never have to cut wood again." The woodcutter grabbed his axe and took a step toward the dragon.
>
> The dragon then raised a claw with huge talons on it and said, "Hold it right there, you SOB. I know what you want to do. You want to kill me with that axe so you can sell my body for a lot of money. Well, I'm telling you that if you take one more step, I'll blow my fiery breath on you and burn you to a cinder."
>
> The woodcutter figured it was no use to try and kill the dragon so he turned back to chopping the tree down. The second time he went to chop the tree, the axe slipped out of his hand and hit the dragon right between the eyes, killing him.
>
> End of story.'

If you haven't quite figured it out, this is a metaphorical story of the possibilities of what can happen if you just 'let go' without trying.

SAINT AND SOLDIER

In the past I have been questioned, with some hostility:

"If you are so Zen, why do you teach violence?"

Great question. The founder of Sikhism, Guru Nanak, summed it up beautifully in his Punjabi teaching:

'Sant sipahi.'

This means, 'Saint and soldier.' Guru Nanak's teaching states that we all have a saint and a soldier in us. However, we shouldn't be so saintly that we are laying down so people can walk right over us like a doormat and become 'repressors'. On the same note, we should be so militant that we are too stern and authoritarian that we become 'oppressors'.

Guru Nanak was alluding to the fact that our inner soldier must stand up to prevent people from walking all over our saintly kindness and compassion when seen as weakness, in the face of injustice.

The secret has always been encoded in the words 'martial' and 'art', where:

- **Martial** means soldier, war-like, destruction and to break.

- **Art** means saint, heal, construction and to create.

The trick is in knowing when to let the justice warrior rise in the face of adversity and injustice, at the right time, with the right purpose and way.

EFFORT IS FUTILE, NO EFFORT IS FUTILE

When you try too hard, you won't get there.
When you don't try at all, you won't get there.

At the peak of your effort, there is a dying. Only then does 'it' happen.

When you are not attached to winning or losing and accept death and defeat as the outcome, then all that is left to do, is to **do your best.**

For when you have trained all your faculties to the level of mastery, anger never arrives and skill stays. There is no opponent that can threaten you, and the images and illusions behind which your foe hides can now be easily foiled because you can recognise all their dirty tricks. Like playing a game of chess, it's as if the pieces start to move all by themselves.

And you can allow the work to be channelled **to you, through you,** like water in a pipe. There is no grasping to the pipe – **it just flows.**

And such is Zen in the Art of Fighting:

A letting go, once you know.

TAKE ACTION AND MASTER YOUR LIFE
ZEN IN THE ART OF FIGHTING

To attain Zen during conflicts in daily life, make these six actions part of your daily ritual so Zen becomes a natural way of being:

1. Centre Yourself

Take long, deep breaths:

- Breathing into your belly through your nose for six seconds – focus on your navel area and make it strong.

- Hold for two seconds.

- Breathe out through your mouth for six seconds – focus on your navel area and make it strong.

- Hold for two seconds.

- Repeat three times.

2. Act with Truth and Love

Whenever someone or something threatens you:

- Take a deep breath to calm your body and mind (refer to step 1).

- Gather your facts first, and get your facts straight. As they say, there are three truths: your truth, their truth and the truth itself – get clarity on all of them.

- Put yourself in your aggressor's shoes to empathise with them and understand where they are coming from.

- Take a moment to process your thoughts carefully. Avoid feeling pressured to speak too soon – take your time, because once your words have left your mouth, you cannot take them back.

- Ask yourself, "What would 'love' do?"

- Then respond with loving peace with calmness, composure and calibration.

3. Perfect Practice Makes Perfect

Cultivate perfect unconscious intelligent responses
by doing the following:

- Dedicate time regularly on pre-set days and times
  to 'practise perfectly'.

- The more you put in, the more you will get out.

- If you fail, be gentle on yourself. Say to yourself,
  "It's OK. What can I learn from this?"

- Refine your practice based on the outcomes
  of your learnings, discoveries and questions.

- Most importantly of all, this is a life-long game
  rather than a short game, so in typical British fashion,
  'Keep calm and carry on.'

4. I Got This!

- Have absolute trust in yourself.

- Say to yourself, "I got this!" and own it!

- Surrender to the process, releasing any
  attachment to expectations and outcomes.

- Allow your intuition to guide you, because
  it is always right, and then just 'Go with the flow.'

- Just do the best you can, and what will be, will be.

- Remember to play, have fun and enjoy the process.

5. Rise and Shine

When you see injustice happening to you, other sentient beings and/or Mother Earth, and you know you can make a positive change, then rise to the challenge:

- Observe the situation swiftly and carefully.

- Orientate yourself within it, to get clarity on what is happening in and around you.

- Decide what action(s) you need to take, taking into consideration:

  - Your congruency, by asking yourself, 'Do my actions sit well with my conscience and consciousness?'

  - Your ecology, by asking yourself, 'Do my actions have a positive effect on myself, other sentient beings and Mother Earth?'

- Act only if the answer to both of the questions is 'Yes'. As Nike says, 'Just do it.'

6. Cultivate Spirit

Rather than only cultivating the body and mind, dedicate time to cultivate the spirit as well by:

- Practising mindfulness daily.

- Then move on to practising guided meditations daily.

- Then seek a guru or teacher, who can light your candle and show you the path towards your own enlightenment with deeper daily practice.

ABOUT THE AUTHOR

SIFU LAK LOI IS A TRUE WHITE-COLLAR WARRIOR.
HE WORKED AS A SENIOR CONSULTANT BOTH IN THE CITY
OF LONDON AND IN WALL STREET FROM 1997 BEFORE
DECIDING TO FOLLOW HIS OWN PATH TO SELF MASTERY.

Loi established the flagship Bruce Lee Jeet Kune Do ('The Way of
the Intercepting Fist') martial arts school in the City of London and
has a direct lineage to Bruce Lee himself. Loi is a third-generation
instructor in Jeet Kune Do, and Executive Advisor to the famous
Wednesday Night Group.

The purpose of Loi's martial arts school is to:

> 'Preserve and promote Bruce Lee's martial art and philosophy
> of Jeet Kune Do, to help define and teach the core curriculum
> – not to confine us, but to liberate us – and to discover our
> personal expression of Bruce's martial art and philosophy.'

His personal mission statement is:

> 'My chief definite purpose is to educate, inspire and empower
> people, so that they can live life to its truest potential... so they
> can align themselves towards their personal liberation,
> self-actualisation and achieve their personal success goals.'

Loi uses Bruce Lee's teachings, fused with his personal development
and elite fitness-coaching credentials, as well as pioneering Dynamic
Framing and Dynamic Anchoring mind-reprogramming technologies,
to cultivate people's lives both mentally and physically through his
process of Experientialism.

Loi calls it... Martial Mind Power.

Loi also holds a Bachelor of Science (Honours) degree in Computer Science/Software Engineering from the University of Birmingham, is a fully qualified NLP practitioner, hypnotherapist, instructor in hypnosis, a chi abdominal massage healer and medium. He is also an associate of the Napoleon Hill Foundation (America's largest personal development organisation, founded by Dr. Napoleon Hill, the bestselling author of Think and Grow Rich), having created their first ever iOS application.

Check out www.MartialMindPower.com for more information.

CPSIA information can be obtained
at www.ICGtesting.com
Printed in the USA
BVHW021557271120
594293BV00022B/150